LIVING ON THE CREST OF THE WAVE

This book is dedicated to my three wonderful daughters, Naomi Finley Griffin, Catherine Finley Buck, Melissa Finley Myers. They are an integral part of the story of this book, and of course, my life. I look back in amazement at their sacrifices and participation in the work, even from a young age.

LIVING ON THE CREST OF THE WAVE

Copyright © 2021 by Ruth Finley. All rights reserved

Cover Photo of wave by Mark Harpur ©All rights reserved.

Scripture references are taken from the New International Version (NIV)

ISBN: 979-8-7486-4808-0 (International Trade Paper Edition)

Printed in the United States of America

The Bible verse I carried in my heart from the time I accepted Christ at 14, is Proverbs 3:5,6 "Trust in the Lord with all your heart and lean not on your own understanding, in all your ways acknowledge Him and He will direct your path." As a person who tried to lean on her own understanding, these verses were powerful reminders.

The verse that Allen and I chose as we began this journey together, was Joshua 1:10 "Be strong. Be courageous. Do not be terrified. Do not be discouraged, for the Lord your God will be with you wherever you go" How often we quoted that verse and certainly God was with us for over 54 years.

- Ruth Finley

Prologue

What does it mean to 'Live on the crest of the wave'?

Allen and Ruth Finley implemented an idea that broke the mold of traditional thinking. It resulted in movements that spawned literally tens of thousands of churches in the most remote areas of the world. This was a 'wave' initiated by God.

'Living on the Crest of the Wave' means being available to God to go against the flow of tradition thinking and traditional methodologies. It means sacrifice: sacrifice of one's own goals, time and acceptance of peers and colleagues. This type of living is done by God-gifted men and women, people who exude the passion and humility of Jesus. It means grinding, detailed pioneering work to open doors to new ideas and a fresh way of looking at the world.

Allen and Ruth Finley are these type people who experienced the exhilaration and the bruises of living on that crest. They were gifted by God yet humble. They were people who could communicate to the least educated, even destitute people and yet sit with presidents of nations and communicate vision.

The huge disparities in wealth between 'christian' sending countries and emerging economies, the largest populations of the world were neglected. Mega churches grew in North America while gifted evangelists in developing countries lacked the most basic necessities.

Allen and Ruth Finley were called and equipped to expand the vision of many to include the thriving and growing churches of the developing world. It was not easy. It involved tremendous effort and sacrifice for the family. The results achieved over the decades by God's grace, have been unparalleled.

This is not a story about an organization or a methodology. This is a story of a family available and willing to be used by God.

– Phil Dempster

LIVING ON THE CREST OF THE WAVE...

1

It all started on a small 200-acre farm in the Blue Ridge Mountains of Virginia, where Allen Finley was born, the last of nine children. His father was a gentleman farmer and as soon as each of the six boys was old enough, they worked the farm – getting up before dawn, taking care of the chores before school and working in the fields. All were familiar with hard work.

Although his Dad had graduated college, he stayed on the farm and kept it going through the Depression and into his 70's. He was a Southerner through and through but neither believed in nor practiced racial prejudice. His lifelong practice, as long as he had health, was driving his old truck from the farm into town, delivering wood to the wealthy homes. If he saw an African American neighbor on the road walking, he would stop and offer them a ride to town.

He also had a wooden plank over the large farm fireplace which read, 'No Smoking' in four languages. His Mother was a nurse and kept the family healthy. Their family attended church on Christmas and Easter. Dad Finley committed his life to Christ when he was 70 while hearing Billy Graham on the radio. Allen's upbringing taught him hard physical work, responsibility and respecting all peoples.

Allen accepted Christ as a teenager, while attending a summer camp. He joined a small Presbyterian Church, where he met an Elder who thought Allen 'had potential' and paid for his college education. During his college years, he majored in History and took courses to plan for ministry. Each summer, he and a team of young men in the ministerial program traveled across the Eastern part of the U.S. preaching in youth conferences and special citywide meetings. One played the trumpet, one led the music and Allen preached. Many made decisions to become Christians.

On the other side of the United States, I, Ruth Goodwin, the middle of three children, lived on a street where Mexicans, African Americans, Japanese and Caucasians resided. They all played together and protected each other during the war, sharing food, gas rations and checking on each other during blackouts. My dad had accepted Christ in San Quentin prison, before I was born. On that never-to-be-forgotten day in prison, his life was totally transformed. I attended church regularly with my father. In High School, I started an after school Bible Study and was active in the youth group at church.

While Allen worked on the family farm, I, with my brother and sister sang in a trio. We were trained by Dad from the time we were little. Dad had a beautiful tenor voice. Dad worked at a plumbing company during the week to pay the bills and would preach on Sundays and Wednesday nights in little churches across the greater Los Angeles area. We would sing in the services before Dad preached. We would then go out to the family car and sleep until we all drove home. No problem leaving three little kids in a car in those days. It was not uncommon. We were never afraid.

My dad's ministry grew and he eventually received a Pardon from the Governor of California. We traveled for meetings in camps in the mountains around Los Angeles, churches and conferences over many years including the Union Rescue Mission in Los Angeles, where my dad eventually served as Director for 20 years. During those years, the Rescue Mission grew tremendously under his leadership. As an aside, he was also featured on two popular TV programs, 'This Is Your Life' and 'To Tell The Truth'.

Between 1950 and 1952, Allen had been involved in mission trips overseas. He directed camps for the children of workers in the pineapple fields in Hawaii and after graduation he spent a year in evangelism in the Middle East involved in directing such camps and preaching in churches in the Middle East.

After two years of college, I accepted a position as youth director at a new church plant in Yucca Valley, California.

Allen was accepted AS A STUDENT at Bob Jones University in Greenville, South Carolina. As a requirement for graduation from Bob Jones University, Allen began to work in the summer at the Union Rescue Mission in Los Angeles. My dad  brought Allen and another young man who was assigned with him to our home for dinner. This was not a new experience. In previous summers, I had met other guys from Bob Jones University. Soon enough one thing led to another and mutual attraction quickly blossomed. We were married in August 1953.

In September of 1953 we joined International Students Inc. (ISI), a ministry seeking to reach for Christ, International students studying in the U.S.

We travelled to Philadelphia for training. During those days we befriended a student from Japan, Kusano-san, at the Wharton School of Business. Allen had many conversations about God with him and we often invited him to our apartment. It was a huge struggle for him to understand Christianity. Months of questions, however, until one amazing day he expressed his desire to be Christian. He said he truly understood and gave his heart to Jesus. Later he shared his desire to go to California before he returned to Japan in order to visit the company that he was associated with in Japan – Ajinomoto.

Those months in Philadelphia were busy and intense. We were in touch with hundreds of students from all over the world. Ten months later we were assigned to the University of California at Berkeley, when Allen became the West Coast Director for ISI. Again, we traveled across the U.S. However, this time we would pull a small trailer carrying our furniture from our apartment.

We remembered the conversation with Kusano-san. We shared with him that we were being transferred to Berkeley, California and asked if he would like to drive with us. He was very excited and most grateful not only to have more time with us, but also he would get to see the United States as few do.

For the next seven years we were involved with ISI ministry in Berkeley. Allen met hundreds of ships at the San Francisco docks, wearing a special badge that gave him permission to go on board to welcome students. We bought our first home and over the next few years we were blessed with three precious, beautiful daughters.

We quickly got involved at a Church, where Allen became an Elder and Chair of the Missions Committee. We met hundreds of foreign students on the campus, at the International House and most often just walking on the streets. We entertained dozens of students in our home from all over the world. Thousands of International students in the U.S. never see the inside of an American home and we changed that for as many as we could. I loved being a Mom and hostess to Internationals. I also look back to this as a time of spiritual growth and struggling well with life.

During those seven years in Berkeley, California, many came to Christ. The first was a young man from Afghanistan. Such a story to tell! Through months of struggle, he never stopped asking questions in his sincere pursuit of God. The day he came to clearly understand his need for Christ, his life was changed. A year later he returned to Afghanistan and within six weeks he was in a plane crash and was the only survivor. As he wrote to us, "How can I explain that I walked away from that crash? Only by God's Hand. God is with me. I am amazed."

As I remember back to those days so long ago, my heart is warmed by the amazing grace of God. Even after these 70 years, the faces of those who came to new life in Christ are in my memory. Those from Japan, India, China, Latin America, Fiji Island, Tahiti, Taiwan, Syria and Afghanistan all come to mind. To this day I am still in touch with three of those former students.

One hot summer day while walking on the streets of Berkeley, Allen said to himself, "that young man wearing a heavy winter jacket is either sick or from Africa". He stepped up and spoke to the young man "Hello! How are you today? Are you a student here?" "Yes I am", said Gus. His smile lit up his face.

As they talked, Allen found out he was from Liberia, West Africa. He said, "Do you know my country?" "Yes", Allen said. "Then you are a different American, as most people don't." They laughed. Allen invited him to the ISI office, where they talked for hours. So much unfolded during that visit, including the discovery that Gus was a Christian and his heart burned for his people in Liberia. As they ended their first meeting together, Allen asked Gus if he would pray before they parted. Well, that prayer vibrated throughout our office, out onto the streets of Berkeley, and began a friendship between Gus and Allen that was to last for forty years.

Gus went on to graduate from UC Berkeley and was listed in a special book published for the 100th anniversary of the University, listing the 100 most outstanding students in the history of the school. He also finished his doctorate degree in ministry at the Reformed Seminary, before returning to Liberia.

Then blew the winds of change. The more we saw students coming to Christ, the more we often heard from those who returned home and the difficulty they expressed in trying to meet Christians in their own areas or locating a Church. Some would face persecution.

At that time one of the local Board Members of International Students Inc., who was also on the Board of a ministry called Chinese Native Evangelistic Crusade (CNEC), requested that Allen have lunch with him. We had never heard of this ministry. The Board member began sharing about this most interesting and innovative mission agency. It was established in China in 1942 and had as its program goal assisting churches and ministries across China. At that time, CNEC in China had 200 workers. Some were teachers, some Seminary professors, and some evangelists.

Their board was looking for their first USA Director. However, at this time, China was inexorably closing churches, expelling missionaries. Persecution was rampant.

The organization believed that the Christians in China could lead their own ministries as equals with Western missionaries. At that time most missionaries were from England and a few were from the U.S. Many were seeking to leave China because of the war with Japan and some already had been forced into internment camps. Although CNEC was not yet known in the U.S., in England, Australia and New Zealand there were laymen who led alliances from their homes. CNEC had set up a United States Board of Directors and had hosted one of the Chinese leaders to come and speak in the U.S. CNEC was looking for their first USA Director.

The Board member put out the challenge to Allen and said, "Will you at least pray about it?" When Allen returned home and we shared our thoughts, the mission seemed to address our earlier concerns of leaders returning home with no support network or financial resources. After much prayer it became very clear that this concept of coming alongside those trained in their own countries, speaking the language, living at the local standard of living, understanding the culture and eager to spread the Gospel, hit a chord in our hearts.

2

We were filled with excitement. In due course Allen accepted the position of General Director, under two conditions. Firstly, the name change to Christian Nationals Evangelism Commission (still CNEC), as the ministry had already spread from China to Hong Kong, Taiwan, Singapore, Malaysia and Thailand. And secondly that the small office which was in the Santa Cruz mountains of California at Mount Hermon be moved to San Jose. Both requests were agreed to.

We knew it was not going to be easy saying goodbye to all our friends but to our pain and shock, our own pastor, whom we loved dearly, did not encourage us and was not happy with our decision.

Disheartened, but believing that God was leading, we continued with our plans. (Eight years later this former pastor attended a meeting where Allen was speaking. He requested to have lunch with Allen and while together he shared he was wrong in his earlier opinion and asked Allen to forgive him. He had driven to the meeting praying he would have the opportunity to speak to Allen directly.)

We sold our home in Berkeley and settled temporarily at Mt. Hermon, a Bible Conference Center in the Santa Cruz mountains near San Jose, California. Here we were, with three little kids, the youngest just under a year. We moved into a cabin owned by the CNEC Chairman of the Board who graciously offered his place for our family. A retired missionary couple who lived in Mt. Hermon had been taking care of the receipts for CNEC donations. The mailing list handed to Allen was in a shoebox. There was one file cabinet with other documents and photos from China and one small desk.

Full of faith and excitement and filled with

confidence that God was leading us, we were sure that the ministry of CNEC would grow. At that time San Jose was the fastest growing city in the U.S. and had hundreds of churches. It was the beginning of the Silicon Valley tech industry and San Jose was at the forefront. We purchased a small home and were able to rent a small office. Allen's Secretary, Pauline Tanji, at International Students Inc. in Berkeley decided to join us. Pauline later married Duke Hatekeda who also served on the international board of Partners International.

Allen began making contacts at various churches. Some of the churches knew Allen's name because he had spoken in many of them when he represented ISI at various conferences in and around the Bay Area. We got involved in the church that our Philadelphia pastor had recommended and they graciously put their arms around us and before long, added CNEC to their mission budget. What a blast of encouragement that was! Out of our church, and others, Allen built a steady and mature local Board of Directors.

We realized all too soon that the major mission organizations and agencies and many churches with strong mission commitments supporting Western missionaries were against the concept of supporting national workers. Many of the pastors and leaders believed you would 'spoil' or make 'Rice Christians' (work for rice) if you gave money to these nationals. How insulting! Was there discrimination alive in global missions? We were not new to mission organizations. We had worked with ISI for seven years, but we soon realized this CNEC concept was not welcome. "The world could be reached only by Westerners" was the leading philosophy. CNEC certainly did not oppose traditional mission efforts. Many of CNEC partners were and are the product of such missionary efforts.

Allen began to attend the conferences for leaders of most Western mission agencies in the U.S. The news was out. The organizations had heard about this 'new' mission called CNEC (in truth, it had been commissioned in 1942). As Allen arrived to register and sign in and meet the various agency leaders, they wouldn't shake hands with him. In the various working sessions, his raised hand was not acknowledged as he sought to join in the discussions. At two later meetings, Allen brought along leaders from Guatemala and Liberia. Even their lifted hands were ignored in discussion groups. With God's grace, Allen never held grudges, was never bitter and he never retaliated. He was tenacious and just kept showing up and presenting the needs of our national brethren!

3

A traditional mission would have hundreds of missionaries on furlough traveling all over the U.S., speaking in meetings, making their organizations known and raising funds. However, this was not possible with missionaries whose home was where they served. Early on Allen knew that this was a huge challenge and CNEC would need to have a new way to make the organization known in the U.S.

After much prayer, we concluded that Allen would accept as many speaking engagements as possible, while still running the mission agency. With God's help, we would find the balance between leading and building a mission agency and our family demands.

We prayed God would use these trips to develop patience in us; increase our faith and bring us closer to Him. *'Many are the plans in a person's heart,*

but it is the L{\sc ord}'s purpose that prevails.'
Proverbs 19:21

We decided that we would pack up our children and commit to driving across the United States every other summer, speaking in as many churches or groups that would invite us. This would include home meetings, women and men's meetings, businessmen's luncheons, Daily Vacation Bible School (DVBS) – whatever! We left no stone unturned. We gleaned contacts from Allen's previous travels and his travels in many States promoting International Student Ministries.

Allen had preached in crusades a couple of summers while in college. This led to contacts with old college roommates who were now pastors. We contacted people on CNEC's mailing list and meetings arranged with those interested. To our amazement, that first summer trip we had a full schedule for the three months.

Friends loaned us a small travel trailer. It is good to remember that there was <u>no</u> air conditioning in the car or trailer. The stops were planned so that the trailer was under a tree if available. We had no GPS and no smart phones. In fact, there were no mobile phones. The girls learned to read maps

The task began of preparing for these trips. Packing was a science. Only take what we will need and not one sock more. However, how many 'more' might we need if someone fell in a puddle? And the rule was to put back what you have used to its exact place when you are finished with it. Nice on paper! We knew from mapping out our trips, (no Google Maps or GPS) some days - especially across the Western desert - we would need to drive 500 miles a day in order to reach our next meeting. Our first stop was in Bakersfield, California, visiting with one of CNEC's board members. They had a swimming pool! What a warm and encouraging start.

Crossing the desert the very next day, a sandstorm came up. Even with dozens of cars driving with headlights on, it was difficult to see the road. We made the decision to stop for the night in the Mojave Desert and that night the wind blew all night like we had never experienced. Our poor little trailer rocked like a boat on a restless sea. Interestingly, the girls thought it was fun!

In the morning we left early and arrived in Phoenix at 6 p.m. It was 100 degrees and the 'coolest' it hit while we were there was 97. We decided we needed a fan for the trailer! Life saver! We found a nice trailer court which turned out to be centrally located though we didn't know that at the time and it had a swimming pool.

It was decided that we would follow this routine in the services: Allen would introduce the family, I would sing, then Allen would speak and show our slides. My repertoire at that time was two songs, so I didn't need to prepare more, unless we were in one church for longer than two meetings! Later the girls began to sing in the services. They learned to sing in Chinese "Laixin Yesu" which translated the song: "Come to Jesus. Come to Jesus, Come to Jesus just now. Just now come to Jesus, Come to Jesus just now." They added greatly to the services and people loved them. I have to smile writing this. Can you imagine that happening in today's churches? What courage and good health God gave us. The girls were troopers and part of the team.

That first meeting the next day was in a church that was started by a layman and had grown tremendously. Standing in front as we drove up was a group of young guys who were in charge of the meeting. They were laughing and soon drew us into what was going on. They were guessing if Allen would look like the picture in the literature they had received. He did!

Entering the church, it was jammed with young couples and children everywhere. Great service, warm reception and the girls had fun playing with all the children. This was a new contact for CNEC.

The Assistant pastor of this church also had a radio broadcast that reached as far as West Virginia. He invited Allen to come on the radio and share about CNEC. The pastor even invited listeners to call the station for more information. That was a first for us.

The CNEC Regional Councilor in Phoenix set up a BBQ on Monday night at his home and invited friends from the area. He also invited Allen to use his office phone, a big help way back then. It was a great evening and at the end they presented us with a box of sweet grapefruit! Tuesday, Allen did more calling. A Chinese man who had attended the meeting on Sunday called Allen and asked if they could meet for lunch. He couldn't express what his heart felt. The amazing reality for him was that a mission existed, dedicated to coming alongside the Christian leaders in their own countries. He remained a donor to CNEC for years.

That evening another donor to CNEC set up a BBQ at his home and invited a large group of friends. We were very encouraged. Wednesday, Allen realized two tires needed to be replaced and the car needed a lube job; we were thankful we were in a large city and not in the desert.

Those days were full, exhausting and encouraging. We were thankful for the swimming pool at the trailer court and it helped to keep the girls happy. We were running out of literature and asked staff members to ship more to Amarillo, Texas. Allen was very grateful to use the Regional Councilor's phone while in Phoenix, so for now, no more hours in hot, smelly phone booths.

We arrived in Los Alamos from El Paso on Saturday night. We had called the pastor and he told us to pull in right behind the church. It was quite amusing to see him bringing hoses for water and an electrical hook up for our trailer.

This location was very convenient. We discovered they had hosted that original Chinese pastor that CNEC had brought to the U.S. many years before.

Our time there was excellent. A lady came up to me after one of the services and we began to talk. Immediately we seemed to relate to each other.

She invited us to their home for a meal. During that visit she shared that Ruth Graham, Billy Graham's wife, was her sister. Her husband worked at the government project in Los Alamos. I knew the story that Ruth and Rosa were born in China. She immediately related to the mission vision of CNEC and subsequently supported the ministry for years. Although this church was not large, in their last annual meeting they had voted to add CNEC to their budget. We had a sense that Rosa may have had something to do with this decision.

NEWS FROM THE FIELD: The ministry is expanding! To God be the glory. Brazil, Guatemala and the Philippines have now been added to CNEC. Income was growing and contacts of friends grew quickly. God was on the move. The crest of the wave was growing faster than we imagined. Churches were being planted and hundreds being baptized. Gus Marwieh reconnected with Allen and sought partnership with CNEC for his ministry in Liberia, West Africa. We were encouraged.

As we drove into Amarillo, Texas, a huge storm caught up with us, and we experienced tremendous downpours, wind, hail the size of marbles, lightning and thunder. The girls were excited. We prayed our car and trailer would be protected from dents. God answered. Thankfully the 28 tornadoes that were predicted turned away from Amarillo.

The meetings in Dallas were larger than we expected; 200 to 300 people at the first church. We were so thankful for the requested literature that arrived in time for our meetings in Texas.

The response of the people lifted our spirits. After the service, their custom was to line up and shake the speaker's hand. We thought we were back in our wedding receiving line again! What a warm and friendly congregation. The pastor and his wife took us out to dinner at some large Texas restaurant, all Texas style – everything over the top. Thankfully we didn't have to be concerned about the girls making noise, they wouldn't have been heard anyway.

We arrived in Longview, home of the R.G. LeTourneau Equipment Company and LeTourneau College. Richard LaTourneau served on the CNEC Board and had invited us to stay in their home. Such a blessing! Thank you, Lord, for this opportunity to rest and be refreshed. Their large dining room held the largest round table I had ever seen, with a huge lazy susan in the middle. The girls loved feeding the ducks and chickens on the back lawn and swimming in their pool.

That first night they invited a few friends to hear about CNEC. Among them was a Chinese student from College. He kept saying "AMEN!" to everything Allen said about CNEC. Thankfully, Richard La Tourneau interpreted it as a solid endorsement!

That first morning, Allen left to speak at the plant chapel hour with 600 men in attendance. In the evening he spoke to the nightshift. There were many Christians among the plant workers and they may have been required to attend! The next day, Allen spoke in the chapel at LeTourneau College. The same Chinese student was in attendance, but kept silent on this occasion.

Allen had spent hours in phone booths making contact with folks from the mailing list. It wasn't any small task standing in those hot, humid and smelly phone booths. However, we had prayed and asked the Lord to use those contacts to encourage people. We had been

always working

going at top speed and yet it seemed we were only scratching the surface. There needed to be a representative for CNEC in the South.

After Nacogdoches, Texas, we spent the night in Vicksburg near the Mississippi river. Alas, we didn't get out the insect repellant soon enough! The next day we were on our way to Birmingham, Alabama when we hit some bad thunderstorms.

There isn't room here to tell in great detail, but there was a small truck parked slightly on the highway, just prior to crossing a small, narrow bridge. Allen steered the car around the small truck as we came to the bridge. A huge tractor trailer entered the bridge coming toward us. Allen knew there was not enough room to pass. He lightly touched the brakes and we started to skid.

We were all screaming. Everything happened in a moment of time it seemed. We have never, ever been so conscious of God's hand on us. Our car was literally picked up and set back down three times as that fast-moving truck passed us. Crossing the bridge we pulled over to the side and couldn't hold back the tears and praise to God for His protection. We were confident at that moment that people were praying for us. How dependent we were and still are, on Him.

Once in Alabama, we enjoyed a nice change in the weather. The temperature had not risen above 71 F after we arrived in the state. The odometer showed we had traveled just over 4000 miles. The experience had been interesting for us to travel through the windy and dusty desert; the West Texas dust storms; extreme heat; and parching winds. The rise and fall of jagged canyons and lazy plateaus was beautiful.

As we moved eastward, we began to see green grass, more trees and summer thunderstorms. We entered East Texas with its wide, lush, green vales, trees swaying in the breeze and an abundance of fresh fruits. Although the weather was hot, most of the homes now and a few cars were air-conditioned. It was rather relaxing to drive through the green countryside in the midst of our hectic pace of meetings, multiple phone calls and new contacts. We had several close calls on the road, but were always so thankful for God's wonderful protection.

Our time in Huntsville, Alabama was interesting. One of the meetings was in a little church way out in the country just over the line into Tennessee. We had not heard of this fellowship before. The church was ready to close three years before, when a young couple arrived to lead the ministry. There were now 130 in the congregation and 60 of those were teenagers. It was a typical country church with the men in overalls and the children sitting with parents through the whole service. Allen felt at home and they immediately responded to him. I guess once a farmer, always a farmer.

One of the farm families invited us for lunch. They gave us more food than we could handle. After lunch we just wanted to nap, but at 4:00 p.m., the pastor announced he had a radio broadcast and expected Allen to speak! The moment the broadcast was over we all jumped in the car and headed back to Huntsville for an evening service. The pastor of this church was a wonderful man. His church had been supporting CNEC. It was an encouragement to be with such a supportive group, one that was already committed to CNEC. They also had a 150-student Christian school attached to the church. They kept us busy the next morning. In the chapel, the students asked us a lot of questions. Our girls enjoyed being around the students.

Leaving Alabama on our way to Atlanta, we drove through the small mountains, covered with beautiful green trees and flowers blooming everywhere. We passed lake after lake of deep blue water with boat-launching sites along the shores. It was all breath-taking. We wished we could have stopped for a while. We found Atlanta to be extremely hot, expressways everywhere, spectacular churches but all the traits of a big city.

A family who supports CNEC invited us to park the trailer in their long driveway during those two very busy days. As soon as we unhitched the trailer, it started to rain. It rained for the whole time we were in Atlanta. We were up early the next morning, as Allen was to speak at Immanuel College. We then headed for Sumter, South Carolina and arrived at dinner time.

We were driving around looking for a trailer space. The one we discovered was owned by a Christian, to our delight and surprise. It was a beautiful court among hundreds of tall pine trees. The owner and his wife were leading a vacation Bible school for the children who lived in the court. They invited our girls to join in and that was a wonderful three days for the girls. Our time in Sumter was outstanding. Seven meetings were arranged where both of us were speaking for three solid days. When we went to pay our bill, we found that our Regional

Counselor for CNEC had already paid it. As a side note, we had now gone many hundreds of miles past 5000.

4

We arrived at the Finley farm in Virginia! It had been three years since the two oldest girls had seen their grandparents. The grandparents were about to meet our youngest, Melissa. What a happy, ecstatic reunion, with much hugging and dancing around. Allen's parents were getting older, so it was a very special time to be together. There were aunts and uncles and dozens of cousins, all gathering to greet us and some meeting us for the first time. There were chickens and horses and cows and acres of farm to run around in. The girls liked this much more than the back seat of a car! Large picnic tables had been set up under the huge tree in the front yard and soon grills were being heated up. Hugs! Family! Tears! Smiles! -meeting babies and little ones for the first time. Thirty of us altogether.

When it was all over it was very difficult saying our goodbyes. We knew there would never again be a gathering like that. As we drove away, we kept looking back, until family became like little dots on the horizon.

The girls began saying they wanted to go home. We told them, yes, we will head West, but there was one more meeting in Colorado. That news was accepted happily and finally we turned toward home.

The next day, we got a call from our headquarters, telling us that the meeting in Colorado had to be canceled. Our hearts were at peace. God knew the limits of our endurance. Pulling into our own driveway in California was special; we were home! All was well. We had obtained new insight into God's faithfulness and protection. We now had to re-capture our lawns, revive our flowers and prepare for the start of school. We rejoined the office staff who had carried on faithfully while we were gone. This fast-growing ministry with all its attendant pressures would now need our full attention.

The demand for speaking at churches continued. It was exhausting for Allen, but encouraging all the same. Some speaking engagements were not quite as encouraging.

One pastor got up at the end of our presentation and said, "What a presentation! This just sounds like something we should get involved in. Ushers, let's take an offering for these folks." Because the girls were always interested in the offerings for CNEC, they told us the offering plates were full. The pastor handed us an envelope as we were leaving which contained $10. $10. ! We assumed the church needed the funds more than CNEC partners. The girls felt the pastor was not honest in either his presentation or his donation. It was quite a revelation for them. There was quite a discussion in our car for the next few miles and years to come.

In most places, we were hosted by loving families who did their best to accommodate a family of five. Sometimes this hosting came with slight variations. In one home, the hostess told Naomi, our eldest, that her bed would be in a closet! A few churches split the girls up with families that had girls the same age.

One home served us liver for dinner. When I didn't insist the girls eat the liver, the hostess gave me a lecture on, "Didn't I know there were hungry children around the world?" Another served us only vitamins in little bowls for breakfast. Another home was near a military base with planes landing and taking off most of the night. The owners were away so the church placed us there. There was no sleep that night as the girls were so frightened, even though we all slept in one bed. The church had arranged that place for two nights but under these conditions, we thanked them and drove away the morning after to our following assignment!

In one home, the couple fought all night in their bedroom and in the morning shared with us that they were discussing a divorce. We listened, we counseled and we prayed with them. Later we received a letter with this message: 'Larry and I wanted to send you a note. The Holy Spirit, Who is in you both, was a witness to us so strongly that we had a brief glimpse of the love and joy that will be ours when we meet Him. Your visit has indeed marked a turning point in our lives. I confess that I was terrified at your coming to our home as I thought you would only see our weaknesses and sins. Instead, you saw only our great need and His love shined through. Thank you for praying for us.'

One large church where Allen would be speaking in Michigan put us in a Sunday School room on the 3rd floor of the building. They had set up beds for us and restrooms were handy. We let the girls run around as they had been in the car for days. At one point we decided to go look for them. We could hear them laughing and talking. We found them playing in the baptistery!

We were hosted by some wonderfully kind, dedicated, sweet Christian families along the way, who couldn't do enough for us. A few took me shopping to get the girls new clothes. Others packed always-welcome lunches for us as we traveled.

Another summer came and a family offered their small travel trailer to us. We found campgrounds where the girls could run around and the best of all were the camps that had swimming pools, especially in the South. Allen used to comment the girls were already in their bathing suits before the car stopped. At one church the pastor said to meet him at the church. There he opened a window off the kitchen area and said to Allen, "Just plug 'er in." We were plugged in at that church for a weekend, which was a nice break from staying in homes.

As time went on, support for CNEC began to grow, as well as the contact list. The mission was becoming more widely known and we felt encouraged summer after summer. However, there came a time when Allen's health began to show the strain he was under. He couldn't sleep and was exhausted. We had a friend in Monterey, California, a doctor whom Allen contacted just to share his concerns about his on-going tiredness. The doctor said, "Take a break and come and stay with us." They lived near the beach.

He took Allen sailing and insisted he have total rest for a week. During those days there, as Allen tells it, he was walking on the beach one day completely overwhelmed with the task of running the mission. He found himself lying flat out on the sand. He prayed, "Lord, it's your ministry, not mine. I believe you called me to this ministry and I can't do it anymore, so I completely yield myself to you and give you the burden." He got up from the sand a new person.

Allen traveled the world many times over, meeting with the leaders of growing, dynamic ministries. He was witness to the unbelievable growth of the church in Hong Kong. He trekked into the scorching jungles of Africa, where the church was exploding and to areas of India, where he experienced mass baptism of hundreds of people in a single service. He saw firsthand the rebuilding of the church in Vietnam, and CNEC was able to come alongside the local church and celebrate the new freedoms in

South Africa. Through all of these travels, he was blessed with good health.

Allen was invited to a large church to be the main speaker at their missions conference. He was invited by the mission team and had not met the pastor. When Allen arrived, they informed him that the pastor wanted to meet him in his study, which Allen did. Allen walked in. It was a very large and beautifully decorated office, with a large cherry wood desk and two leather chairs sitting in front. On the pastor's desk was a two-pen holder, with gold pens.

The pastor and Allen talked for a few minutes and then the pastor reached over and picked up one of the gold pens, pointed it toward Allen and said, "Don't you know you ruin nationals by giving them money? You spoil them." Allen leaned forward and took the other pen out of its holder. Holding it in his hand he said, "Pastor, I know about your fine ministry here, your mission commitment and I notice that you have a beautiful office, with high quality furniture, everything you need as the pastor. I don't believe that you are spoiled. We work with pastors around the world who have nothing. Some are meeting under trees."

There was total silence. They sat for a few minutes. They shook hands and Allen left. Later Allen received a letter from the pastor, apologizing and saying that he was wrong and God had really spoken to him. He wanted Allen to know that their church would be totally behind the ministry of CNEC.

Around this time, Allen was speaking at a missions conference where Ken Taylor, the author of the Living Bible, was in attendance. He came up to Allen at the end of the meeting and said that he was deeply touched by Allen's message and the vision of partnering with Christian nationals around the world. He invited Allen to come speak in the Chapel at the Living Bible headquarters in Illinois.

I remember as if it was yesterday. We were on one of our summer trips when we arrived at the Living Bible Headquarters. The Chapel was full of staff. Ken took Allen to the front of the room and I stayed at the back with the three girls. Allen was exhausted and feeling discouraged with the rejections and the climate of mission agencies and some large churches. We were all tired. Ken Taylor got up and said, "Staff, I want you to sit up and really listen to this man this morning, because his organization is on the crest of the wave of a major change in Western missions."

Allen sat up, squared his shoulders with his spirit lifted, and began to speak. I was sitting in the back with tears in my eyes so grateful for this encouragement for Allen. From that day on, Living Bible supported the ministry and Ken was a great encourager to Allen, introducing him to other funding possibilities. It goes without saying, Ken's endorsement gave CNEC a real boost.

Ken Taylor was not the only significant leader to back CNEC and encourage the work. Dr. Ralph Winter, a renowned missiologist and founder of the U.S. Center for World Missions was quoted "CNEC/Partners International is the Cadillac of mission agencies working with indigenous ministries". These endorsements provided tremendous impetus to the work.

Many other missions leaders befriended Allen and encouraged him in the work. Leaders of the Evangelical Foreign Missions Association (EFMA) and the International Foreign Missions Association (IFMA) Wade Coggins, Carl Henry, Jack Frizen and Bernie May of Wycliffe remained friends for years.

As CNEC continued to grow, with partnerships in more than 60 countries, Allen urged the Board to again change the name, this time to Partners International (PI), which they agreed to do. Allen was commissioned as President. This was a much more inclusive name and more truly expressed what partnership was all about.

5

The U.S. office staff was growing. It was soon obvious that more space was needed at the home office. Allen began to look around San Jose for a building. He noticed in the paper a large building for sale, near the airport and the growing tech businesses of Silicon Valley. He liked what he saw from the outside. The building was close to San Jose airport. It was a 10,000 square foot building, and even contained a dark room for developing photos and a recording studio, both built by the previous owner. He called that man and asked if he could see the inside. Within minutes the owner arrived.

They walked through the building and Allen saw immediately that here was the potential for a growing ministry. Before they talked price, Allen asked the owner if he could share with him what the business (ministry) was that he was involved in. "Yes, of course," was his reply. He was an older man and seemed in no hurry. Allen later learned he owned many properties in San Jose and was eager to sell this large building.

Allen began telling him about the million-and-a-half refugees who had fled out of China into Hong Kong. Many were highly educated doctors, pastors, teachers and engineers. Thousands were families with children. Hong Kong could not handle that many people flooding in, so high rises began to be built for people to live.

Among the refugees, some of the pastors began setting up cardboard tents on the hillside to start churches. Teachers began gathering children for simple schools and the doctors set up clinics, with medicines the HK government gave them. "Just think," he said to the owner, "a million-and-a-half people coming over the border from China into Hong Kong!"

Allen continued telling him how the refugees began to form committees and made contact with the HK authorities. The authorities were sympathetic to the plight of the refugees. It was discovered that the roof of these new high rises, once fences were built around the roof, could be used as schools for the refugee children. Thousands of children lived in those buildings! The Government gave permission to start Schools on the Roof Tops and for many years, Partners International supported thousands of children through the 'Support a Child' program. Eventually, there were seven such Roof Top Schools led by Christian teachers and principals. "We have ministries in 50 areas of the world;" Allen added.

The owner was quiet. Finally, he spoke up and said, "This is most amazing. My wife and I came to this country from Italy, with nothing. God has blessed us beyond our dreams. Just yesterday, my wife said to me, "You know, I think we should be supporting some group or children that are needy". If you don't mind, I would like to go home and share with her what you have told me and we can meet back here tomorrow."

The next day, Allen again met the owner. He said he had talked to his wife and they decided together to <u>GIVE</u> the building to PI. From a tax perspective, it would benefit him! That day at staff prayer time, there was excitement, a few tears and a sense that God was on the move. That building allowed the staff to grow and the ministry to expand around the world.

In the next dozen years, the staff grew to 57. A local TV program was produced in the building, interviewing some of the leaders from around the world who were brought to the States to share about their ministries. The printing press and production of all the publications for Partners International was located in the new facility.

Videos were produced highlighting the testimonies of various national leaders. A volunteer staff of 20 were regularly in the mailing room helping wherever they were needed. The building was also used for gatherings of pastors and donors, giving them an opportunity to meet many of the nationals who were coming to the U.S. for speaking engagements.

6

Allen and Ruth in the new office celebrating 25 years at PI

DADDY'S HOME! Allen had been traveling overseas most of this year, meeting with the leaders and boards of the growing partnerships across the world. We were all excited! Praying and strategizing. Where to this summer, Lord? It was clear, without a doubt, that we should go North to Northern California, Oregon, Washington and

Canada! Why? We knew we would have the opportunity to visit Mr. and Mrs. Fred Savage who ministered in China. Fred was an engineer and his wife a missionary. It was their involvement that began the ministry and organization called CNEC, now Partners International.

They were a great encouragement to the Chinese workers. To meet them was an experience we didn't want our girls to miss. The president, Dr. Jepson of the first U.S. Board of CNEC also lived in Seattle. He was a doctor and highly respected in the Northwest, especially among Christian businessmen. He had 'ploughed the ground' and opened the area, building support for the Chinese evangelists. He presented CNEC to churches and individuals for years in the Northwest. He was the one who had arranged to bring the Chinese evangelist connected with CNEC to the U.S. many years earlier.

Dr. Jepson passed away a few years later but some on that original U.S. board living in the Seattle area, continued to work for CNEC, even though elderly. They were very keen to help in any way.

Those original donors and churches who had not been contacted in many years would be our focus. We were thankful for those remaining board members still living in the Northwest. Our thought was to contact them, call some of the churches and donors still contributing and see what develops. Within three weeks, we had a full itinerary to cover three months travel, starting with the first meeting just North of San Francisco. We knew God was in this.

On this trip we had a station wagon and no trailer! We followed our normal packing routine except we added sleeping bags for all of us. Our first meeting was in the home of donors, just north of San Francisco. We soon discovered the traffic was backed up for miles because of a San Francisco Giants game! Could we get across the bridge in time for the meeting? We did! The hosts' home was beautiful, with lots of room for everyone. It included a backyard with tennis courts and a swimming pool. Being that close to San Francisco brought cool temperatures from the foggy ocean breezes. However, the host had heated the pool to 88 degrees so any of the children of invited guests could swim. Well, you can imagine who the first three in the pool were!

The hosts put on a BBQ well attended by many from the church with the pastor and his wife. There was lots of food and a friendly group of about 40. It was an unusual arrangement. The host had done an excellent job of preparing the guests about the gathering. We were introduced and then our host encouraged people to take turns sitting next to us to ask questions then move on!!

We were greatly encouraged. After the feasting, everyone sat around while Allen spoke for a short time and showed slides on the ministry. There was a great response and the pastor asked Allen to come back and speak in their church at a later date.

That night our sleeping arrangements were most interesting. Since it was a large home and they had six children of their own with their own rooms, the girls were given sleeping bags on gym mats and we were given a folding bed that sagged in the middle. When we woke up the next morning, Allen said, "Have you ever slept on a fence?" We couldn't stop laughing. In fact, in all the years of travel, we have learned to laugh over sleeping arrangements. Melissa, being the youngest, usually got the most interesting setups. More than once she slept on two arm chairs pushed together. She thought they were special. Sunday morning we were up early and were served a huge country-style breakfast with luscious blackberries picked from their backyard. "Lord, give us strength for today."

It was only a short drive to the next meeting at the home church of the then Chairman of the CNEC Board of Directors. We were looking forward to seeing them as well. We arrived Sunday morning at 8:20 a.m. for an 8:30 morning service. It was a large church, so the girls and I settled into a pew and Allen disappeared behind the platform with the pastor. The morning service was on the radio and Allen would be preaching.

About three minutes before the broadcast, Allen came into the sanctuary and quickly walked back to me. "The trio that was supposed to have the opening music hasn't shown up. The pastor wonders if you could sing a song. Give your music to the organist! I jumped up, ran to the car to get my music, and handed it to the organist, all before the red 'Ready to Record Light' came on. When I returned to the pew, the girls were anxious and I was shaking.

Sunday afternoon, an hour further up the highway, we were to have a service at 6:30 pm in my aunt and uncle's church. (My uncle was the pastor.) It was wonderful to see family. What a service! The church was packed. Apparently they seldom had a missionary speaker. The sanctuary was built in the late 1800's and had a very visible and beautiful baptistery with artwork at the front. There were old-fashioned carved wooden pews, very pretty arrangements of flowers from my aunt's garden in three or four vases across the altar, and an old organ and piano at the front of the sanctuary.

Sixty percent of the congregation were young people. My cousins, who played the trumpet and trombone, led the music, accompanied by both piano and organ, and they really lifted the rafters! Our hearts were moved. Allen spoke and showed his slides. The people pledged ongoing financial support for eight children in addition to a wonderful offering.

We were with family, so I had the opportunity to pack a large lunch for us to take with us the next morning as we left. We were excited to have some time at the Giant Redwood National Forest, where we stopped for a picnic. Oh, the greatness of those magnificent trees! They take your breath away! Psalm 96 says, 'Sing to the Lord a new song. Declare His glory among the nations, His marvelous deeds among all peoples. Then all the trees of the forest will sing for joy.' For a time, we stood in that forest and couldn't speak.

We had hoped our next stop would be the Sequoia National Park. However, there was a lot of construction on the road and it slowed us down.

We were determined to visit the park if we could. Confused by all the construction, Allen spotted a policeman sitting in his patrol car. He asked the policeman the best way to get to Sequoia Park. He looked in the car at all of us and said, "Follow me." We never thought we would have a police escort! Sequoia Park is a beautiful place, near the Pacific Ocean. There was a zoo, a picnic area and a playground, so it turned out to be a great spot to walk around after being in the car all day.

We arrived in Eureka, California and called the Browns, our hosts, to get directions to their house. This couple had supported CNEC for some years and had heard Gus Marwieh from Liberia, a few years back. They had a three-bedroom home and six daughters. Getting ready for the evening meeting at their church, Mrs. Brown announced that they were planning to leave their girls at home and could our girls stay home as well? You can imagine nine little girls dancing around the room, so very happy that they could stay home and play!

I looked at Allen, and he looked at me with a smile that said, "It's up to you". I picked up my purse and walked out to the car. The meeting was well attended, with much enthusiasm. Allen spoke, showed slides and I sang. A man came up to us and said he was the pastor of another church and wondered if we would be willing to come to their home with the Browns and visit for a while. It became another late night and when we returned to the Browns, we could hardly walk across the floor with nine little girls sound asleep in sleeping bags.

7

Our next stop would be Brookings, Oregon. Mr. Kerr, a CNEC Board Member, lived there and had planned meetings for us. He owned a huge logging company. We arrived at their home at 2 p.m. and were received with a truly loving and warm welcome - like a burst of sunshine after a rain. Their home sits on a hill overlooking the Pacific Ocean. Their swimming pool was built inside a heated building so they could swim year 'round. Their house had a basement apartment, which they turned over to us. It was wonderful to be able to do laundry. Their grandchildren were around all the time and were really nice kids. They came and welcomed the girls to swim. There was also a missionary couple from England with two little girls, staying in the home. We formed quite a group.

The pastor of the Church where we were to speak, invited all of us for dinner at their home. They had seven children. Another elder in the church, plus some others were also invited. It was a lovely time but a lot of kids.

Mrs. Kerr made an appointment at a beauty salon, thinking this would be a lovely gift to me. She drove me to the shop and introduced me and then left. She told me someone else would pick me up, as she had a meeting to attend.

When I was finished, the missionary from England picked me up in the Kerr's car. Before I could put my seatbelt on, the car started to move, the driver slammed on the brakes, and I was thrown head-first into the windshield. The impact was so hard that my head cracked the windshield and I was knocked out. I was not able to attend any of the meetings and felt sick for three days.

We prayed and trusted God to protect me. Mr. Kerr was extremely upset and felt very badly about it all. He wondered why the missionary hadn't told them he didn't know how to drive an American car. We left two days later and Mr. Kerr followed us in his car for an hour to be sure I was okay and not in need of medical intervention.

That night we stayed in a small motel on our way to Eugene, Oregon. We were all carrying in our luggage, when I heard Allen screaming, -"Ruth, come quickly!" He had closed the door with his foot, but it caught his thumb! In this particular car, you had to open the doors from the inside. By the time I could open the door from the inside his thumb was a mess. I put his hand in a motel ice bucket.

Allen can take a lot of pain, but now the pain spread up under his arm. I called the motel office to see if there was a doctor or nurse on call. We needed to make sure we were treating it properly. They told us that there was not anyone available and that we better go to the hospital. So at 9 p.m. Allen took off by himself and followed the directions to the hospital while I stayed with the girls at the motel. After a wait in the Emergency Room, the doctor (he was very nice) said he would have to drill a hole in the nail. He did and the blood erupted out, but relief came!

It was midnight by the time Allen got back to the motel. The girls were asleep and I was sitting on the edge of the bed praying: "We have every confidence in you Lord that we are in your will. I've hurt my head and now Allen's hurt his thumb, all in one day. Please teach us what we need to learn and thank you for your presence at a time like this. You are faithful!" The next morning Allen's thumb looked better and the medicine the doctor gave him was helping dull the pain. We left for Eugene.

We arrived in Eugene, OR to the home of the Heriders. Mr. Herider is on the Board of CNEC. Mr. Herider was quite elderly at this time and had difficulty walking, but they would not hear of us staying anywhere else. They welcomed us as family and it wasn't long before the girls were calling them Gramma and Grampa. We were smothered in love. They had a small trailer at the side of their house, so Mrs. Herider put boxes of toys in there, which became the girls own private play area.

 The girls couldn't have been happier. I began to notice that the girls soon discovered that "Gramma"

Herider would give them anything they asked for! A stop was put to that quickly!

That evening, a Chinese professor at the University invited Allen to speak in his home to a group of Chinese students. There were 40 students that attended and it was one of those meetings of kindred spirits. What an evening! The questions and sharing went on until midnight. The students were blown away by Allen's understanding of China and very interested in how CNEC works. Allen was greatly encouraged.

Once we left the coast and came inland, we became aware that this area of the country is known for problems with hay fever. That first night Allen coughed a lot. The symptoms were initially mild with no sneezing or watery eyes. The congestion seemed to settle in his chest and affected his voice. He had a difficult time taking deep breaths. Mrs. Herider took the girls and I sightseeing while Allen stayed back dictating for hours to the staff at the headquarters in California. There was a time before email ! After we all returned Allen looked at our schedule and realized our next meeting was at 3:00 p.m. It was already 2:10 p.m. but the meeting was in another town, but not too far away!. Mrs. Herider said "leave the girls!"

We quickly changed and grabbed the literature and slide projector and arrived at Miss Hanson's home at 2:50 p.m.. She was a retired missionary from Korea but stayed very involved in world affairs and missions. She lived with her sister, a retired teacher, in a lovely home with gorgeous antique furniture.

Another older lady who had supported CNEC attended as well. When she walked in, she had the CNEC PRAYER MANUAL in her hand. (-CNEC produced a Prayer Manual for many years with the photos of the national workers and prayer requests for that particular worker or region.) Allen and I felt as though we were among saints. Twenty women were sitting around the living room, including her pastor and his wife.

Allen spoke and showed slides. The questions showed clear knowledge of CNEC and that went on until 5:30 p.m., closing with a time of prayer. We seldom experienced the depth and passion of that prayer meeting. Their prayers lifted us to Heaven. We were convinced at that moment that people like this were used of God to build and protect the ministry of CNEC. We felt refreshed in our spirits. They had planned a special dinner, unknown to us. We called the Heriders and they said, "no problem everyone is happy". By the time we arrived back to Heriders later, the girls were asleep.

That night Allen began coughing and was up a good deal of the night, but he had to get up early for a meeting at Miss Chang's home. We had deliberately planned the next 3 or 4 meetings in retirement homes around Oregon. Some of CNEC's significant donors in the Northwest were folks that lived in these retirement communities.

The next day, we would meet this powerful Chinese Christian lady that we met at a conference in Indiana some years back. She worked in China for 35 years and just loved hearing about the ministry of CNEC. Her family had placed her in a Lutheran Home in Salem, away from anyone she knew and without Chinese fellowship! She radiated Christ and her welcome to us brought tears. I asked her if she was ever lonely and she said, "I have Jesus!"

She had arranged for Allen to speak in her small church near where she lived and after the service she invited the pastor and his wife to join us at the famous Strawberry Fields. We never knew Oregon was such a berry country. We picked huge, delicious berries and then she took all of us to a lovely restaurant for lunch. Back to the Lutheran Home Miss Chang guided the girls and I to the Library and Allen to another room where he could rest before the 4 p.m. meeting in the Chapel..

At 3:45 p.m., the Chaplain asked if I could sing at the service and provide the piano accompaniment as well. I said "I would be glad to and that our girls would be happy to sing as well." He was thrilled. He said the residents would love seeing the girls. I went to the car to get my music and returned to the gorgeous, carpeted Chapel. It indicated the services were probably very formal.

I soon discovered the Chapel had only a huge organ! I play piano but not an organ and certainly not one like this! I sat on the organ bench and started praying! -"Oh Lord, make this sound ok! Help me not to mess up and distract from the message and songs!" I began to pull and push some of the stops and determined I would not use the pedals! Somehow with God's grace we got through the service and Ms. Chang couldn't have been more thrilled. The residents loved the girls singing and were full of hugs at the end of the service. We were grateful to have been here, if for no other reason than to experience the joy of being in the presence of this saint, Ms. Chang.

We jumped in the car and arrived in Portland in time for the evening service at First Baptist of St. John. There was also a later meeting where Allen was to speak to the youth. The Youth meeting was great and the kids asked a lot of interesting questions. The pastor and his wife invited us to their home afterward and showed real interest in CNEC. It was an encouragement to later learn they put CNEC in their budget. They invited us to spend the night with our sleeping bags, however, Allen was struggling with hay fever and coughing. We declined and decided to go to a motel where there would be air conditioning and see if that would help relieve his suffering.

We drove back to the Herider's on Monday morning and I was able to do some laundry. However, the greatest gift was Mr. Herider purchasing two new tires for our car! Thank you Lord! We had a home meeting at the Herider's that night and it was well attended. The folks were quite interested. Heriders having the meeting in their home was a strong endorsement for CNEC.

Allen continued to struggle with hay fever and sleeping through the night was impossible. We decided he should go to a motel again with air conditioning to see if he could get some sleep. During the night, he continued to get worse and couldn't breath. He got up and drove to a hospital. The emergency doctor told him there was a constant stream of people coming in this time of year with breathing problems.

The Doctor checked him out and said he wasn't getting any air in his lungs. He gave him a shot of adrenalin and ordered another shot that would "help you for 48 hours until you can get out of this area." He went back to the motel and slept until 10:00 a.m. When Allen awoke he came to pick us up, pack the car and we left for Salem, Oregon. Through all of these challenges, God had given us inner peace.

We received encouraging news from the headquarters. Income was growing at 20% and the mailing list was growing at a steady pace. Thank you Jesus! Use all of this for your glory and the extension of your work across the world through CNEC. The partnership ministries around the world were growing rapidly, especially church plants, agricultural projects and medical clinics. These were so desperately needed in India, Liberia and Nigeria, countries of CNEC focus at this time.

The next morning we left for Centralia, Washington. The Carlsons would be our hosts. We knew their name because they regularly contributed to CNEC. It was interesting upon arrival to discover they lived out in the country where they owned and managed a Retirement Home for 22 residents. The Carlsons were from Sweden and couldn't do enough for us while we were there. They had a swimming pool, so the girls enjoyed that so much! Around the facility , they worked 6 acres of land, from which they had plenty of vegetables as well as a few chicken's. The girls loved feeding the chickens.

The meals they served were abundant and delicious. They seemingly couldn't do enough for us. We looked forward to the meeting that evening when others from the town were invited to join the residents. Allen shared and showed slides and the girls sang. After the service, Mr. Carlson, a very distinguished man, got up and told the crowd, " I first heard of CNEC many years ago from Dr. Jepson, the original US Board President and I've been completely sold on this mission ever since." Well, we couldn't have had a better recommendation!

Many Support-A-Child cards were taken as well as a substantial offering. The next morning, Mrs. Carlson told me that she had made an appointment at a Beauty Salon for me. (She must have thought I needed help!) It was one of those incredible interventions that God brings along every now and then. The young gal that was assigned to me, asked me "where are you from and what brings you here?" As I shared, she began to open up and tell me about her life and struggles. The owner, who was a Christian, told me later that she couldn't believe it when she heard the conversation, because she had tried to talk to the young gal before with no success. She even came and sat down beside me while I was under the dryer (that dates me) and continued to ask spiritual questions.

The next morning we left for Enumclaw, Washington for a home meeting with Mrs. Glassco. I had corresponded with her for about a year, as she had requested the CNEC Prayer Manual. She planned to have a home meeting and we had agreed. We followed her directions and discovered she lived at the base of Mt. Rainer. The home meeting was to start in 20 minutes and we were not sure if we would make it. However, we pulled up with 10 minutes to spare to this run down, renovated cabin.

This lovely young woman came out of the house, her face radiant and greeted us with such joy. Soon, we were introduced to her 10 children (one with learning disabilities) all of them smiling. Soon she had tears in her eyes as she said "I invited many people but no one has come. I'm soooo sorry! Please forgive me. I'm so glad you are here!" We assured her we were happy to be there even if no one else came.

We walked inside, the floors were bare and there were two bedrooms, no curtains at the windows and only enough chairs for the family. A broken down piano with half the keys not working, sat in the corner. After a short conversation, Allen asked Mrs. Glasco if she had some blankets and a sheet. He hung the blankets over the windows and hung the white sheet on the wall and set up the projector. The girls sang a couple of songs and I sat at the piano with the broken keys and sang "God gives more grace when the burdens grow greater, He gives more strength when the labors increase, to added affliction, He adds His mercy, to multiplied trials, His multiplied peace. His love has no limit, His grace has no measure, His power has no boundary known unto men, but out of His infinite riches in Jesus. He giveth and giveth and giveth again."

I could hardly keep back the tears, but I was able to finish. Allen, showed the slides and to our amazement, Mrs. Glassco, kept recognizing various nationals, as she had prayed through the Prayer Manuals. She was sooo excited and kept commenting. All the children sat attentively.

We then turned to Mrs. Glassco and asked her to share with us her life journey. She seemed eager to share. She said she was 28. Her husband was a mechanic and a drunkard. There were days when she didn't want to live, so one day, she walked out to the edge of the mountain, beyond the cabin, thinking she would end her life, when God met her in her deepest and personal need! At that moment, she fell on her knees and cried out to God and promised the Lord that no matter what life would throw at her, she would try to bring glory to Him. She claimed the promise that her husband would come to know Jesus and all her children would love Jesus."

"It hasn't been easy," she shared, "but life in Jesus will get you through!" She continued… when she got up from her knees and looked out over the expanse of Mt. Rainier, God showed her the world. She stood stunned! Her 'world' was so small, but God began to expand her world! She started in a limited way to pray that many would come to Christ. It was at that time, she ordered the CNEC Prayer Manual and used it every day out on that mountain.

We went to minister, but we had been ministered to! We left there with a lump in our throats. Allen and I didn't speak going down the mountain. Is it any wonder God blesses CNEC, with folks like this praying for us! After returning home, I was scheduled to speak at a Women's Conference in the mountains. At the end of one of the sessions, I told the story of Mrs. Glassco. After the service 3 women came up and asked if it would be acceptable to send clothing for Mrs. Glassco's girls. I contacted Mrs. Glassco and she was very touched by the offer of these women. She sent the sizes of her daughters and later these women sent 4 boxes of clothing! Mrs. Glassco was thrilled and deeply grateful. She said the girls couldn't stop dancing around the house! How wonderful when people respond to God's prompting.

In the middle of this particular trip, I would like to take the opportunity and pay tribute to our 3 girls, Naomi, Cathy and Melissa. They have done a magnificent job. They have contributed more to our ministry than they realize. I know the Lord has been with us and people have been praying because the girls could not have stood these years of tight schedules and traveling without the prayer covering. Constant meetings, up late, early rising, singing at almost every meeting, meeting new people constantly and adjusting to new circumstances. They never complained, especially over any food they might not like. It is truly amazing. I know it wasn't easy. There is no question that they added to our ministry. We are so proud of them and thank God for each one for their own talents and personalities.

8

After Eugene, our trip continued northward. We arrived in Seattle and drove to the home of a long-time donor, Mrs. Jackson. We were to be in the Seattle area for a week. She lived in a typical home on the hills surrounding Seattle, where the gardens are beautifully kept with flowers among the rocks. She showed us around the house and handed us the keys to her home. She said to call her if we needed anything, that she would be staying at her daughter's. We couldn't believe it! How lovely to have one place to stay during our time here.

We spread out and it took us one whole day just to clean the station wagon. Unfortunately, I was quite sick with a flu – caught somewhere along the way. Allen was able to cover the meetings and took the girls with him so I could rest. Wonderfully, Mrs. Jackson's son was a doctor. He came twice to check on me and gave me some medicine which helped with my recovery.

In a couple of days we were to take the ferry across to Port Angeles and then would have a four- hour drive to Gallam Bay, where meetings were scheduled in a church that faithfully supported the work of CNEC. There had been no one representing the mission there in years.

We arrived after what seemed like a long time. When we drove off the ferry, we heard strange noises coming from the car. We found a gas station with a mechanic who would check out the car. He told us it was the water pump. Allen asked if he could fix it and he reluctantly said that no, he could not. "I don't keep pumps around and the only guy in town who carries them is closed. But I know the guy so I can call him at home and see if he would be willing to open up and fix your car." He did and the car was repaired in short order. We couldn't believe it!

The mechanic told us it would be a three-hour drive to Gallam Bay! It didn't look that far on the map. It turned out to be four hours and a very windy and long trip. We arrived there at 11:00 pm. Now we knew why no representative had come there.

The elder who arranged the morning and evening meetings for the next day welcomed us warmly. He and his wife wanted to stay up and talk. The Elder and his wife had a huge house so we were very comfortable there. Those living in that area seldom saw visitors, especially any special speakers or missionaries. We then realized Gallam Bay was at the end of the world! We could look across the Bay and see Canada, so it certainly must be the end of the world.

We were introduced to a young man who was in the Air Force. He was staying with them for the weekend. His father used to be the pastor of the church. He seemed about 20 years old and was at a difficult time in his life, a time of questioning his faith. He had come to visit for the weekend to see his old friends. He immediately felt relaxed and enjoyed chatting with the girls as he shared with us that he had four younger brothers and sisters.

Allen had a couple of conversations with him and we were not sure if he would attend the meeting, but he joined us. Because of questions from the congregation, they wouldn't let us leave after the service. It was another very late night. However, we were aware of God's evident presence.

The young man asked if he could ride back with us to Seattle and we agreed. While on the ferry going back, he had some good talks on the deck with Allen. He expressed his desire to reconsider his faith and when we arrived at the dock in Seattle, he didn't seem to want to get out of the car. He just kept on talking. All at once, Melissa, our youngest, leaned over and kissed his cheek and said, "Goodbye, brother." He had tears in his eyes. The girls often wondered what happened to him.

9

The next morning we packed the car and left for Vancouver, Canada. This would be an opportunity for us that we had waited years for. We were meeting Mr. and Mrs. Fred Savage, now in their later years. Fred was an engineer and his wife was a missionary when they met on a ship headed from England to China. They eventually married. Fred began to see the gifting of many Chinese Christian leaders and believed wholeheartedly in the concept of CNEC. He was on the original Board in 1942 when CNEC was organized.

He personally supported some of the Chinese workers out of his own salary as an engineer. The war with Japan was causing great harm. The Savages were put into an internment camp. They were finally able to leave China and fled to Hong Kong with thousands of refugees. The Savages became the liaison with the CNEC U.S. Board. Allen met them many times in Hong Kong as they coordinated the ministry there. After their retirement they settled in Vancouver, where their son and daughter lived.

To spend time with them and to sit at their feet, was as if sitting in God's presence. True saints! Amazingly, they had looked forward to our visit for years. Their basement was stacked with boxes containing the history and photos of the ministry in China from the very beginning. They entertained us beautifully, like Chinese do, always serving small sandwiches, tea and cookies.

Days were spent with Allen and Fred in their basement, learning of those early CNEC years, marking the names on the back of pictures of those pastors, teachers and workers who had been left behind when China closed. Allen kept the pictures under lock and key for 30 years. Great care was taken not to publish the photographs as many of these workers feared for their lives. Many had been imprisoned and even killed for their faith.

One afternoon, we had the joy of seeing one of the International Students that had come to Christ during our years in Berkeley. We had kept in touch with him and he was now a pharmacist in Vancouver. It was such a blessing to find him still walking with Christ. A year after our visit, he was killed in a car accident.

Mr. Savage had arranged a special meeting with Chinese business leaders on Sunday afternoon. He shared with Allen that some of those attending were important people in the Vancouver government. I stayed back with the girls. When Allen drove up in our old station wagon, he thought he should park on the street! The old car was a little out-of-place in that wealthy neighborhood.

His host, Mr. Wong lived in a 4 story mansion! There was a circular driveway and chauffeur-driven cars.   Allen saw a man motioning to park in a spot for the "honored guest". Allen wondered how he knew who he was. Later he was told that Mr. Wong had told everyone to come at 2:00 p.m. and he asked Allen to come at 2:30, so everyone was already inside.

Mr. Wong , a lawyer, had a high position in the City Government. Allen later shared he thought Mr. Wong used the occasion to pay back all his social obligations because of the people that were there! The Ambassador from Australia; the Chinese Consulate General; top business associates, to name a few. In all, there were 60 guests.

When Allen realized who his audience was, he changed his approach and showed his slides. He opened the meeting for discussion and was impressed with the questions, especially about the CNEC ministry in Hong Kong among the refugees. CNEC was building many schools and some on the rooftops of the high-rise buildings.

Mr. Wong was thrilled with the presentation. Everyone was invited into the drawing room for tea, as Mr. Wong announced that there would be a bowl on the table for any donations to the ministry. Surprisingly, it was the lowest offering of the trip.

Upon Allen's return, we rushed to the evening service at the Metropolitan Tabernacle, Fred and Geraldine Savage's church. The service was to be broadcast on the radio. The pastor was very enthusiastic in his introduction. After the service, everyone was invited to go downstairs to see the slides. We thought no one would show up, but 150 stayed for the slide showing...real interest.

The next day we came through the Canadian Rockies on our way to Kelowna, British Columbia, the farthest point North on our trip, we found that the man who had arranged the meeting for us had gone to work on the night shift! The Pastor of the Church had left on holiday! It was an interesting two hours trying to find out what we were supposed to do. We finally located the Church and learned we were to stay in the pastor's home right next door to the church.

The church secretary walked us over and handed us the key. We entered, looked around and thought this would be great as we had the house to ourselves. However, when we inspected the bedrooms there was a note on the pillow which read "Use front bedroom only". Evidently the man who arranged the meeting didn't tell the pastor we were coming as a family! In addition, everything was turned off except the electricity, no heat and no toilet paper! We made the decision to put our sleeping bags on all the beds and hoped the pastor's wife wouldn't mind!

 Allen then walked next door and knocked. A nice lady answered and Allen asked if she had an extra roll of toilet paper we could use! She was shocked that they hadn't left any TP and gladly gave Allen a couple rolls!! (I Hope you think this is funny, because we certainly did!) By that time it was too late to eat, so we walked over to the church and set up the projector and laid out the literature. Soon people began arriving.

A good crowd attended and greeted us warmly, including a missionary from Latin America. It turned out he knew the CNEC national Director in Guatemala very well. The missionary said to Allen, "How do you get your wife and kids to travel with you. My wife and kids refuse to go with me so they all go to their grandparents when we are on furlough!"

A few people found out we hadn't had dinner, but no invitations were given for dinner or breakfast. As we drove out of town we were grateful for all the hundreds of folks that had graciously hosted us. We were not that far from Grand Coulee Dam, so we decided to treat the girls on a tour. It was amazing because, as it happened, the water was rushing over the spillways, so the noise and beauty were magnificent.

10

We arrived in Spokane, Washington the next day and called our contact. He informed us a secretary at the 4th Memorial church where we would be speaking, would be turning over her apartment to us.

She couldn't seem to do enough for us and filled the refrigerator. There were 3 rooms and two very large walk-in closets. The girls chose to play and sleep in those closets. The Savages had given the girls each a Chinese doll, which they cherished, so they spent a lot of time playing in those closets. To our surprise and delight, there was a public swimming pool just 4 blocks from where we were staying. The pool had 5 life-guards and was well supervised. The girls were delighted!

Our contact person in Spokane aired a radio program, Vision Radio. Allen spoke on air on three different days. He had spoken every day and sometimes twice a day. There is a King's Men group from the church where Allen spoke on the Sunday. They met on Thursday nights with more than 100 men in attendance.

In the morning we received a call from the Director of a children's TV program requesting that the girls be on the program and sing their Chinese song. The girls were excited. The format is more like a Sunday School program and is taped on Saturdays and viewed on Sunday mornings. We saw the program on Sunday on TV. It was a wonderful experience for the girls.

4th Memorial is a great church. It reminds me of the church I attended as a young girl. Dr. Vernon McKee was my pastor. This church funded CNEC for a long time. It had been 8 or 9 years since any CNEC representative had been there. Sunday afternoon Allen spoke to the High School kids at a service. Then at 7 p.m. he spoke in the main sanctuary and showed slides. The church was packed! The choir loft was jammed with young people who could really sing! After the meeting, a family took the girls and I, plus three other families to their home for something to eat. The pastor took Allen to the College-age "sing."

On Tuesday, our host directed us to a Laundromat down the street. I took all our laundry down there. When I arrived, the lady in charge took all our laundry and commented, "You must be Mrs. Finley." Yes, I said. She said please give me your laundry and I'll have it ready for you in an hour. When I went back everything was folded and ironed! What a lovely surprise. When I left, she said, "Please bring your laundry in before you leave, so you can travel with everything clean." Wow! Another burst of encouragement.

On Tuesday we were to meet Mr. & Mrs. Griffiths who were hosting a meeting in their home. They were Presbyterians and their pastor attended. The Griffiths had learned of CNEC from Dr. Jepson many years before and they were looking forward to our coming. There were 16 folks that joined us in their home. A good meeting and warm fellowship.

The Griffiths had a large vegetable garden in their backyard that Mrs. Griffith tended to at 71 years of age. She tried to sell the vegetables in front of their home to make extra money. Mr. Griffith was hit by a car a few years back and had difficulty walking. In their home was a 94 year-old man that they cared for. This also brings in some funds. Their daughter, brain damaged at birth, lived in the home.

Naomi was quite fascinated by the old man; she sat and talked to him before the meeting. I noticed a well worn CNEC Prayer Guide on a stool in the kitchen area. Mrs. Griffith had prepared a light dinner. Everything was fresh from her garden and a baked cherry pie right from the oven for us. We ate outside on the patio under their lovely trees. It was a precious evening and visit.

Perhaps because we had been so busy traveling and in meetings, Allen and I reacted emotionally to the Griffith's generosity and hospitality. At times we couldn't keep back tears especially during the prayer time at the end of the meeting. The joy and sweetness that flowed from this couple touched us deeply. We felt as though we had walked among saints.

We left Spokane on Friday and headed to Colfax, WA. Here we were scheduled for meetings at the Onecho Church. We had known of this church for a few years and were looking forward to our time there. This farming community was active and involved. All the farmers in the congregation had more than 1200 acres or "you are not a farmer if you have less!"

This is modern farming! They all grew wheat and had the latest equipment and lived in lovely, large homes. Allen, raised on a farm, said he had never seen anything like this! We were to go to the Morgan's home first. We hadn't been there 5 minutes when their kids saddled up their horses and had our girls riding off. Allen was one of the first 'kids' saddled up and riding!

Our visit was only an hour old when Mr. Classens came and led us to his farm. We planned to stay with them until the following Monday. They were harvesting, so we all had our turn riding in the combines. What an experience!

The combines were glass enclosed and air conditioned. They dump the wheat into the back of huge 5 ton trucks into bins in the barns where it is stored. They offered Allen the job of driving one of the trucks and he loved it. After he had dumped the wheat into the bins, too much wheat ended up on the ground. They gave Naomi and Cathy small shovels and they scooped up what was on the ground. It gave them the sense of helping. Melissa was bobbing up and down in the truck with Allen, blowing the loud horn!

The Onecho Church was very unusual. It was just a country church with about 150 members. They were very mission focused and had a mission budget larger than the operations budget of the church, including the pastors salary. Amazing and very committed to CNEC. I think all 150 attended the meetings with such appreciation and enthusiasm.

On Monday morning when we got up, we noticed that Mr. Classens and his son were not at breakfast. We finished packing and started out to our car. We discovered they were both working on our car. Mr. Classens and Allen had earlier discussed the issues with the car. They came to the conclusion our car needed a generator and a muffler. They rose early, drove to town and brought back what was needed. The repairs were finished before we had to leave! We were stunned and deeply grateful. What special servants, totally aware of others' needs.

11

There is excitement as we began another summer ministry trip. A lot of praying and planning had gone into this trip. CNEC continued to grow under God's blessing, adding daily to those who are stepping into leadership overseas.

Churches were being planted and thousands were coming to Christ. We felt blessed to be part of that Family of God! So we carried on, in partnership with our brothers and sisters across the world. We prayed for protection as we believed that the summer's trip will advance His work.

There was a lot of country between California and Texas! Praise the Lord, on this trip we had air-conditioning! We had not planned to travel to Texas again, however, God seemed to have put together the itinerary. A few churches in Texas requested us to return. We arrived in Dallas to find that the church had arranged a motel for us. A motel with a pool! The girls helped unload and were in the pool in minutes. What a treat it was after a long journey in the heat.

We were up early on Sunday and ate breakfast at the motel with food I had brought along. The church is large, with a huge educational building next to the sanctuary. Allen was to speak in different areas, first to the Juniors, Junior High, High School kids and then the College class. The girls and I were waiting for our orders, when someone asked if I played the piano. So I was ushered off to the Primary department while the girls were taken to their age classes.

The room was full of 100 or more kids and there were no music books on the piano. I was sitting there thinking, "This is not happening. I can't play without music." I look back on this experience and have to laugh because God must have taken control of my hands, as I was able to get through all the songs they were singing. I have no idea how except that somehow that large class had piano accompaniment to their singing!

A short time later, the pastor came and asked me to come downstairs to the large Women's Sunday School class where I would be introduced. There were probably 150 women there. He introduced me to the leader. The class was obviously in a heated discussion about something or other so I sat in the back waiting. The discussion was concerning the end of the world and some were excited about a radio broadcast they had heard that very morning saying that there was going to be a terrible earthquake in San Francisco and Northern California was going to drop into the sea! After this statement, three or four ladies chimed in that they hoped that evil California would drop into the ocean!

After being introduced, I didn't have the heart to tell them I lived in the San Francisco area. However, I took time to thank the church for their support of CNEC and their supported national worker, Peter Pan in Malaysia. My heart was heavy as I sat in that class. Is this the Church of Jesus Christ? Lord help us! Later on in the sanctuary, Allen was introduced and the pastor announced that he was Director of

CNEC and that he and his family lived in California. I didn't look around.

Allen's message that morning was powerful. His message cut across the gloom and doom which had gripped the Church. "God is alive and will build His Church and the gates of Hell cannot stop it," he preached. This is a church that says a lot of "amen's". There were few that morning. The pastor rose and asked people to come forward after hearing the message. Twelve people came forward and all waited to talk to Allen, after the closing prayer. The general comments were, "We were getting so discouraged by the news and found ourselves bitter with our lack of love." It was quite a service. When we got in the car the girls said, "How come people don't have a chance to come forward to receive Christ in our Church?" That certainly gave us food for thought.

That night at another church near Dallas there was an excellent crowd. Allen asked me to sing. I met with the pianist and she said she only plays in the key of C! I beg your pardon? She transposed all the hymns into the key of C.

Well, I can't sing in the key of C. So what would we do? I could have accompanied myself, but I prefer eye contact with the congregation, so at the last moment, Naomi very bravely accompanied me. Such a willing spirit! I was so proud of her. Afterwards, she started shaking as that was the first time she had played in public. We were encouraged with the response of this church.

We then moved on to Louisiana and this time we were heading to a Presbyterian church. They were vitally interested in CNEC and had a potluck dinner sponsored by the men in the church. After dinner the girls played their melodicas, I sang, Allen showed the slides and gave a short message. In closing he asked if anyone had any questions and for the next 45 minutes he answered one question after another. It was all very encouraging. The Church put us in the Manse, because the pastor and his wife were in the Holy Land. Their two sons, 16 and 20, were there to show us hospitality. These guys couldn't do enough for the girls! They were jumping at each girl's needs. It was quite funny. Never mind the girl's parent's needs!

In the morning they prepared a wonderful Southern breakfast of fruit, home-cured bacon, eggs, biscuits, grits and coffee. After breakfast, to our surprise, they cleaned off the table and sat down with us to talk about missions. What a blessing. We felt encouraged. Their Dad had a beautiful sports car, so the older boy drove the car out of the garage and invited the girls to take a ride. It was agreed we would follow them to the Interstate and then the girls would get in our car. It seemed fun for all of them.

The next stop was Jackson, Mississippi. The church again put us in a motel. We were grateful for some 'down' time. The pastor came to pick up Allen and showed him the church. We all went for a quick dinner before the evening meeting. The girls played the melodicas and I sang. Allen spoke and showed slides. After the service we were delighted to learn that six folks attending were from another church across town. They were on the CNEC mailing list and heard we were speaking. We had a great visit with everyone afterwards. All-in-all, it had been an encouraging meeting.

Somewhere in Mississippi, Naomi, Melissa and I picked up a bug with very, very sore throats and head colds. We tried to treat ourselves but by the time we got to Sumpter, we were really sick. We called our contact and they put us in a motel. They thoughtfully arranged for two rooms, so the sick ones could stay separately. Thankfully we had a free day, but the next night we were to speak to a group called Faith Missions Group made up of businessmen who came from different churches but who all had hearts for missions. It was just an incredible group of men with great passion for world evangelism.

They had been supporting CNEC so we were really looking forward to being with them. The group met in an upstairs room at a bank and it was one of those meetings of kindred spirits. It was such a praying group and very encouraging, with lots of fellowship. The girls played their melodicas[1]. Allen shared and showed slides followed by a great question time. The group knew many of the CNEC workers by name. They prayed over us before we left and our hearts were touched. Allen asked if there was a doctor we could call to get some medicine for us, as Melissa was getting worse. Allen went to a pharmacy where the doctor had sent a prescription for penicillin and that immediately made a difference.

We arrived in Harrisburg, North Carolina around 4 p.m. The pastor and his wife were friendly and earlier invited us to stay in their home. Upon arrival they informed us that bats had descended on their house and the house would have to be gassed! Thankfully they had arranged housing for each of the girls in a home with a child their age. That turned out to be very enjoyable for the girls. They

---

[1]

The melodica is a free-reed instrument similar to the pump organ and harmonica. It has a musical keyboard on top, and is played by blowing air through a mouthpiece that fits into a hole in the side of the instrument. Pressing a key opens a hole, allowing air to flow through a reed. Wikipedia

assigned Allen and I to another home owned by a lovely couple.

The next morning at the church, Allen spoke to the young adults' class and I spoke to a combined primary to 8th-grade class. It would have been very difficult to talk to a group with such an age span, but thankfully I had the girls go with me. They taught the kids a song in Chinese, "Come to Jesus". The kids loved it.

The morning service was warm and welcoming. After church, each girl went with her host family for lunch. The hostess where we stayed fixed a Southern meal. Now if you're not familiar with a Southern meal, here it is; – two meats, three vegetables, homemade biscuits, two salads, potatoes and a big homemade pie. When we finished, it still looked like no-one had eaten from those large bowls! This is the way of the South and it is delicious. Whenever we were not scheduled with someone, we tried to eat very little to compensate for these huge feasts.

The next stop was Gaffney, South Carolina, the home of Fred Manning. Fred was the Southeastern United States representative for CNEC. Fred wonderfully represented the ministries of CNEC throughout the South for many years.

We were scheduled to speak at the Limestone Presbyterian church. We were housed with the Carrs, a couple we had stayed with before. They have a large, beautiful home and we all had our own room.

That night the church was packed. The pastor was very warm in his introduction. It was a good service. Then the pastor announced that everyone was invited to the Carrs' home to meet us. The whole church?! Yes, it seemed so. The gathering was in their backyard and the folks kept Allen busy answering questions until 11 p.m. Many of these folks already supported children through CNEC, but more Support A Child cards were taken and our hosts took five cards, one for each of their five grandchildren. We were refreshed in our spirits and healthier when we left.

Georgia was our next stop at the Toccoa Falls Conference grounds where Allen was to share in some of the meetings for three days during their family conference. It was a camp solely for pastors and their families. It provided great exposure for us to new churches. Naturally, there was a lot of 'shop talk' among pastors between meetings! It was 97 degrees and it never did get any cooler!

Our hosts put Allen and I in the boys dormitory. During the school year the Toccoa Falls Bible College meets on these grounds. Each girl was placed with her age group and did everything the others did in that group.

It was a nice break for all of us to be separated. However, there was no relief from the heat and humidity in that brick dorm. Allen said it felt like Liberia, West Africa and I agreed. They kept us busy and Allen spoke every night. One night they set up the projector outside so Allen could show the slides to all the campers. It was a very responsive crowd.

Next stop, Charlotte, North Carolina at Thomasboro Presbyterian. This was a large and beautiful church with a congregation of 650. To our surprise the pastor was a classmate of Allen's. We stayed in the manse with the pastor's family. They had an evening service in the basement of the church and the meeting was packed out. The girls sang and played their melodicas. I sang as well. Allen shared and showed slides, presenting the need for sponsors of the Support A Child program.

The pastor did something we had never seen before; after Allen spoke, he got up with one of the sponsor cards for SAC and said, "My wife and I have just signed up to sponsor a child and we want to encourage you to do the same." There were many cards taken that night because of the pastor's bold step but the encouragement to us personally could not be measured. He admitted to Allen he had never done anything like that in his church before. The next morning the pastor took Allen over to the Church and showed him around and introduced him to the church secretary – and challenged her to take a SAC card, which she did! Thankfully, Allen 'just happened' to have a card in his pocket!

Sunday morning arrived and our next stop was in Lenoir, NC. Allen pastored Lenoir Presbyterian Church in town as well as a country church in Setzer Gap each Sunday evening during his senior year of college.

This was a stop we were really looking forward to! The family in Lenoir, who had housed Allen every Sunday through the year he ministered, were truly like family. They loved Allen as their own and were thrilled to meet his family. It turned out they were very discouraged about their own Presbyterian church. We then learned that morning service at their church had been cancelled. We were happy we could encourage them.

In the afternoon, we arrived at the little country church in Setzer Gap. It was packed out with many who were there when Allen was their pastor. What a homecoming. So emotional! Many of the men gave Allen country hugs and lifted him off his feet. The ladies cried seeing him and there were many kids who were little and now grown, who might not remember Allen, but they had heard his name over the years. They were excited to see him in the flesh at last. There was such excitement in the air! It was truly a family reunion.

They had great difficulty finding a pastor out there in the country when Allen was in College, so when he came, they really loved Allen. It was hard to get the meeting started. Everyone was crowding around the family, reminiscing and showering us with affection.

These were hill people. Some had no shoes on and clothes that didn't match, but could they sing! When I got up to sing, I looked down at a young man sitting among all the boys and he pulled out a switchblade and had a smirk on his face. I was a little concerned.

Allen got up to preach and decided to give his testimony first, since there were so many kids in the audience. He then preached a challenge to world missions. All the kids went silent as God's presence was unmistakably there.

The layman leading the service knew Allen well and had given Allen money to cover his gas costs when he was a student. He stood up in front of the church and with tears said, "I have never been so moved! Imagine people in Africa and other countries begging for the Gospel!" With that he hung his head and wept and finally uttered, "What can we do! What can we do!"

People across the room started crying. Everyone was silent for a long time. After a final prayer, the first to step up to talk to Allen was that young man with the knife. He shared he was a new Christian and was struggling with his old life in a gang. He said he worked to support his family, so he wasn't able to finish high school but he was challenged by hearing Allen's testimony. He asked for prayer so he could change his old habits. Allen prayed for him. We found it difficult to pull away from these folks.

They just didn't want to let Allen go. We needed to head for Virginia the next day.

It had been almost six years since our family had seen their grandmother and extended family. Not everyone was able to join this time, however, there were 20 of us on the farm so it was a happy time for us all. Allen's mother was not in good health. In fact, we had hurried to have this visit, as the family was moving her off the farm to one of his sisters in Richmond. We treasure in our hearts her wonderful smile. We remember how she kissed our hands and cheeks. We carry in our hearts the memories of her prayers and faith through the years.

12

We arrived in Washington, DC in time to locate the Grace Baptist church where we were scheduled to have the evening service. They meet early so folks can get home before dark. The church is in an area that was burned down during the riots. Many businesses are still boarded up, some next door to the church.

The church leaders determined to stay in that location so the congregation was wonderfully integrated. Their service was also a blend of ethnic groups. We

were richly blessed worshipping together.

We were told that the Sunday School has more African-American children than white children, but again, greatly blended. The pastor wanted to have the service in the sanctuary and then move to the basement for Allen's slide show and for the girls to sing. There was a good crowd, with mostly children and young people.

We were impressed with the attitude of the leaders. They just persisted despite the problems. We were not sure anyone would stay for the basement service, but it seemed no one left. We had a wonderful service and were thankful that five child sponsorship cards were 'adopted'.

We stayed in DC, lodging with Allen's brother and his wife. On Monday, Allen spent the day at the Evangelical Foreign Mission Association and the State Department working out some issues. The CNEC Partner in Nigeria wanted to work together with the Red Cross. Enquiries were made to secure help from the Red Cross in some of the disaster areas of Nigeria where CNEC worked. Allen made several good contacts. For my part, I stayed back with the girls to catch up on laundry, drying and ironing.

Tuesday, we had promised the girls that we would take them to tour the White House. We were standing In line with hundreds of people when Allen looked down the line and saw our friends from Joliet, Illinois whom we had stayed with many times when speaking in their area. They had become like grandparents to our girls. They were on vacation and here we all were with thousands of other people. The girls were so excited!

We then went to the Capitol and picked up passes for the Senate. We met many Senators. While waiting in line for lunch in the Senate Cafeteria, we met two men from Thailand and a man from Liberia. What excitement, when Allen spoke Thai to them. The man from Liberia was beside himself when he learned that not only did we know about his country but that Allen had been there twice! They wanted to eat lunch with us.

On Wednesday, Allen spoke to the very large Christian Businessmen's luncheon in Washington, DC. They showed great interest in what he had to say. It was an encouragement to Allen. That evening we were delighted to have been invited to a gathering to honor Dr. Christie Wilson, a highly respected and well-known missionary who had worked in Afghanistan for many years and with whom we were friends from our Berkeley days. It was such a joy to see him again.

As we were mingling around the room, I saw a couple across the room and our eyes met. We couldn't believe it when we saw each other! Here were the sponsors of my Church High School group! They lived and breathed missions. They often had us pray for the world. Many times over the years, I thanked God for them and their influence on my life. They eventually joined USAID and worked in Iran and Afghanistan for many years. It was an amazing connection after 25 years.

13

We were now slowly heading west. We left DC and were on the road to Ohio, when Naomi and I again didn't feel well with terrible sore throats. Thankfully we were able to refill the prescription from back in South Carolina and we both began to feel better.

Lynhurst, Ohio was our destination. We planned to stay with old friends we had met the last time we were there, when we spoke in their Church. Our meetings this time were at the Mentor Baptist Church, first on Saturday for a church picnic and then on Sunday morning. Our hosts turned over the second floor of their home to us. They had filled one of the rooms with Barbie dolls, with all their clothes and dozens of toys that their girls had outgrown. Also, they had a freezer downstairs full of popsicles. They told the girls they could help themselves. Not too healthy, so that came to a stop quickly. In another room they had set up a desk with a typewriter for Allen. He rented a Dictaphone so he was able to get a lot of office work done. There was no internet in those days.

Years before, Allen led a week of meetings at this church. They did not have a building at that time. The pastor set up a tent. God blessed that week and the church was planted. Allen and the pastor had become good friends and many of the people remembered Allen as well. We were looking forward to being there. The Saturday picnic was a great success with about 200 people attending. The current pastor asked Allen to bring a devotional at the picnic so he spoke on 2nd Samuel 18, about Cushi running with the message of Absalom to David. The people were very attentive for being at a picnic and the message was quite applicable in that setting. During the picnic Allen had the opportunity to ask a few folks about the former pastor and to his shock, he was informed that the pastor had an affair, was subsequently divorced and out of the ministry. Allen was shocked and felt ill.

On Sunday, we arrived at the church early. As we were getting out of our car, a man in shorts and sandals stepped out from behind a large tree, walked over to Allen, and without a word reached out and hugged Allen and cried. Allen recognized him immediately. They both cried. It was an incredibly touching scene. I took the girls on into the church. It was not easy for Allen to preach that morning, however, God blessed the service. Allen said as sad as it was, he was glad the former pastor had come to see him.

To our surprise, the evening service began somewhat differently. The pastor announced that a few people who knew Allen from those early days wanted to say something. One lady got up and shared that she was in the hospital with cancer and Allen visited her and prayed for her. It meant so much to her, as he didn't know her at all. She never forgot his visit. A couple were separated and seeking a divorce when Allen talked and prayed for them individually and together. Here they were, still together and happily married.

One lady shared that she hadn't wanted the baby she was expecting and Allen had counseled her and helped her. She had her daughter come up to meet Allen. Another young woman got up and said she was learning to play the piano, but was scared and too timid to play in public. Allen encouraged her and asked her to play in the tent meeting. She shared she is now the church organist and is married to one of the Deacons. That brought a laugh from the congregation! Five others got up to share that they had accepted Christ in those tent meetings. One by one they shared. It was a humbling experience and also very encouraging. It was a reminder that we never know how God will use us, but how important it is to remain available to Him.

14

We left the next morning, heading West! 'California here we come, right back where we started from!' We made a stop in Indiana at Cedar Lake Conference, where Allen needed to attend a Board Meeting of an ordination group. The breezes off the lake were so refreshing and the girls enjoyed swimming there. When the director heard Allen was on the grounds, he asked him to preach that night and Allen asked me to sing. In the morning we continued our journey.

Somewhere along the road in Kansas we started having problems with the car. We were in the proverbial middle of nowhere when the car slowed to a stop. Thankfully, we were coming down a hill when Allen exclaimed loudly that there was a gas station down there. "Lord, please get us to that station!" We coasted right into the station before the car completely stopped. We all sat there wide-eyed. It was a miracle!

Thankfully there was a mechanic. He checked the car out and told us one of the gears had gone out. Then he said it would be three days before he could get that  particular gear. Oh no! the girls yelled and all our hearts sank. I don't know if it was because of the girls or for what reason, we decided to go next door to a small shack of place to eat dinner. None of us was hungry at that point, but we tried to eat something. We talked to the Lord and all agreed there was nothing else we could do but trust Him in the good and bad.

We all walked back to the garage and the guy came out and said (even now recalling this makes tears come to my eyes) "I went in the back of the shop where I keep a bucket of oil for various parts of cars. I reached down in that bucket and pulled out a gear that fits your car". Miracle! Even the mechanic thought it was a miracle. In just under three hours we were off in the night praising God and singing. We asked the Lord to please help us find a motel before it got too late. A motel was on the horizon. Oh, the faithfulness of God!

15

The year is 1972. Can it be? Our final trip! Naomi, our eldest, has been chosen from her High School Sophomore Class for a study tour of Europe this summer. We are proud of her and will miss her while we travel.

This particular trip will be different from past ones. As well as Church services, our schedule this year contains two large and significant conferences, in Pensacola, Florida and Ocean City, New Jersey.

Arriving in Houston, Texas, we drove into the worst electrical thunderstorm we had ever encountered. Because we couldn't see the road, we finally had to pull over to the side of the road, along with about 300 other cars! We eventually found our host's residence, quickly changed and followed the host, a medical doctor, to the church.

It was an excellent service with God's blessing. Many people had never heard of Partners

International. They were very warm in their response and interest. It was nice as they had planned a reception for us after the service and the folks asked many questions. We were grateful they had refreshments as we had not had any dinner. It was late when we returned to the home where we were billeted. We quickly realized the place was extremely interesting and might I say, unique!

The most interesting things were the six antique grandfather clocks in one location, with ten more clocks in the hallway. Persian rugs, a pump organ, a cabinet full of various sizes of pewter and copper pitchers. There were also antique lamps and footstools.

The girls were upstairs in a four-poster bed and we had the downstairs bedroom. Unfortunately, not until later did we realize that six of the clocks chime through the night at different times, some very loudly and all with different tones. We were tempted to turn them off but decided against it. In the morning, we had breakfast at a table that was a meat butcher block, eight inches thick. It was all very fascinating!

After breakfast, it was on to Pensacola, Florida. This would be a week of youth missions meetings. We were housed in a very large home, where six teenagers were also staying. It was quite an experience! The kids were not rowdy, they just didn't want to go to bed. A few of them played guitars and wanted to sit around and sing. This was great for them, but Allen had to speak and teach an elective class on Missions the next morning and each morning during the week.

The first night of the conference, there were some 200 teenagers in attendance; such energy and great singing. The days were completely full with activities, including time at the beach. The white sand in Pensacola was beautiful.

The home where we were staying was some distance away from the church where the conference was held. We ate all our meals at the church. A rule was announced that the kids had to bring with them everything they needed until after the night meeting. No one was encouraged to return during the day to where they were housed and no transportation would be available.

The kids could walk to the beach in the afternoons. Can you imagine high school girls, usually not knowing what they are going to wear until three minutes before they get dressed – or after having been at the beach for a few hours - adjusting to this rule? It was pretty interesting but also encouraging as we never saw any kids fighting the system. Having been in leadership, we knew this rule was part of the plan of discipline. This was a youth missions conference. We were thankful this rule didn't apply to us. If we had a free hour, we went back to the house and took a break.

Our two girls really enjoyed the week and talked about that conference years afterward. Dinner was at 6:00 p.m. and vespers at 7:30. Allen shared the vespers with Dr. John Oliver, a pastor from South Carolina whom we greatly respected.

Allen was to speak in his church the following Sunday, and in the well-attended class he taught on missions in the afternoons. God met us in these evening vespers. We got to know a lot of the kids and we appreciated the opportunity to have time that week to engage in the lives of these young people.

At the end of the conference, 55 of the young people came forward to dedicate their lives to full-time ministry and four came forward to accept Christ for the first time. Typically there were lots of tearful goodbyes as we prepared to move on. All in all, it was a good week.

16

Atlanta, Georgia was the next stop. Allen was scheduled to speak at two services on Sunday morning. The pastor was young and energetic and had a great group of ruling Elders. They made a decision the previous year to use 50% of the church budget for missions and Partners was part of that. It was very encouraging to be there.

We spent a few days with Allen's sister and family in Aiken, South Carolina. We then drove on to Augusta to John Oliver's church, First Presbyterian. It is an historical church. The main structure is like a museum; even the pews have the names of past Presidents on each row.

This church was liberal for years and it was nothing short of a miracle that this young evangelical pastor was called to this church. Many of the older people who have attended the church for years were not quite sure what was happening, especially when they saw hundreds of college and university students and young families attending.

The usher took me to the Woodrow Wilson pew, but it wasn't long until an older couple came and informed me that this was their pew, indicating that change is hard. Of course I smiled and moved. Before I moved, the husband informed me that Woodrow Wilson's father was the first pastor of the church.

What a service! With that huge pipe organ, the hymns reached the rafters! God was in this place and many thanked Allen for his message. Afterwards, he stood with Pastor John at the back of the sanctuary. John Oliver and their missions committee had already put in place a large missions budget which included Partners International.

We had to keep on moving, so onward to Norfolk. We crossed the Chesapeake Bay through an extremely interesting series of tunnels and bridges 20 miles long.

Allen received an urgent message from the headquarters that he was needed for some important meetings and decisions. So we drove to my cousin's home in Salisbury, Maryland which is on this same peninsula. Allen flew to California and I stayed with the two girls. Allen flew back to Salisbury but surprised us by bringing Naomi back with him!

The timing of Allen being in California was perfect, in that Naomi's arrival from Europe would coincide with Allen's trip back. So the girls and I drove to DC and stayed the night with Allen's brother and his wife. We then drove to National airport to pick them up. It was wonderful to see Naomi get off that plane with her Dad. Thank you, Lord! She talked all the way back to New Jersey, telling us about her time in Europe. We loved hearing all about it. In fact, she talked so long she had laryngitis for a few days.

Our next meetings were in Ocean City, New Jersey. The pastor of this church was a visionary. The Church is less than two blocks from the beach, with a congregation of around 200 and their mission budget is $110,000 a year. Ocean City is much like a ghost town most of the year. However, during the summer, hundreds of thousands visit the area to enjoy the beautiful beaches. Almost every home was made into a guest house. There were hundreds of homes such as these and many motels along the beach.

The pastor shared his vision with the church about having some influence on the beach crowd. Afterward, four couples made the decision to buy one of those houses on the beach so they could potentially reach some folks for Christ.

The guest house we stayed in had four bedrooms upstairs available to rent and living quarters downstairs for the Christian family who managed it. In addition to their desire to reach young people for Christ, the basement hall at the church remained open daily during the summer, staffed and supported with church funds, ready to help anyone who walks through the door. There were games and basketball hoops and places to sit and talk.

We were given one of the rooms in the guest house. There was one bathroom. These accommodations were wild… so many people and so few (1) bathrooms. People from every background and age group stayed there. One room was rented to two older ladies, another one to two young college girls and the third room had two high school guys. Our family had the fourth room.

Allen was the speaker on Sunday morning and had various other responsibilities until Wednesday. After that, we would be on the road again. He slept in a single room with our entire family. We moved the one single bed against one wall in a corner. We always carried tacks with us as well as tape, so we took one of the blankets off the bed. Thankfully it reached across the corner for some privacy for Allen. But we still had only one bathroom for four women, Allen and the rest of the house guests!

It became a funny contest (not so funny…really) as to who would get to that one bathroom first! Melissa decided to take it upon herself to be the 'toilet lookout'. She found a small place in the hallway where no-one could see her but she could see if the bathroom was clear. We would hear

"Empty!" and one of us would run. Then the next person would call out "Empty!" This whole week felt very much like some of our experiences traveling in remote areas overseas!

On Sunday, there were 1,000 people in the church service. God's presence was evident. Every piece of literature we had put out was taken. Only God knows the impact but we all said that these were rewarding days, even with all the challenges. The beach became our saving grace out of our small room.

We had the opportunity of talking to many people and had a great appreciation for the impact the vision of one church can have. As we left in the car, we acknowledged that we still loved each other. That was a bit of a challenge, considering the closeness of those few days!

We were heading West, but first Naomi wanted to visit Wheaton College in Wheaton, Illinois and Northwestern University, and then one more meeting in Iowa. We asked the Lord to protect us and cause us to bless someone on the way.

17

When I think back to those summers and reflect on those trips, it was not easy! It was always hard work breaking new ground. Many times we became exhausted, discouraged and disappointed. Often we felt it came down to "could we make it one more day?" We were traveling all day trying to get to meetings on time and preparing spiritually on the way.

God was faithful! We continued those trips every other summer for many years until the girls were beginning teens and wanted to be with their friends. I can truthfully say, during all those summers, we never heard them complain. They were troopers and especially interested in how much was in the offering for CNEC! As Allen had reasoned at the beginning, this constant traveling in the U.S. and overseas gave our family time to be together. The girls had the opportunity to see much of the United States!

As we sought to make CNEC/Partners International more widely known over the years, looking back I'm struck with the reality of God's amazing protection, enabling us to continue even through difficult health issues and challenges of circumstances. His amazing love! His amazing grace!

I've come to realize what He desires is not talent or personality, but a willing spirit to be available. With His help, we could overcome the difficulties as long as we stayed in His Presence.

 I think back to the thousands of people we were able to bless just by showing up. Beyond the preaching and singing, we were in a position to touch many folks who needed some encouragement, a smile, a listening ear. For that, we give God all the glory.

Epilogue

Naomi, gifted in administration and a woman of prayer, now lives in North Carolina near me. She loves to garden and her yard shows it! She cares about the underdog.

Catherine is retired from teaching in the area of Special Needs High School Students. This was a challenging assignment, but one she loved and dedicated herself to. She has 4 children and 4 grandchildren. She lives in Wisconsin.

Melissa, a gifted Bible teacher, loves the Word of God. She has an autistic son, who has become our family historian.

Allen passed away in 2006, after a battle with cancer. Not once, did he say "why me". He was at perfect peace through the pain and treatments. He often said, "God is always at work whether we see it or not". How true.

We received emails, cards and letters from around the world during those difficult days. What an encouragement they were, a taste of heaven to come. I always loved what the indigenous leaders said of Allen " He was the first American Christian leader that listened. He was more interested in how God was leading us."

CNEC BOARD

The early board of CNEC were critical to the growth and impact of the ministry. Early board members established the foundation and provided the seed money to grow the work. Many gave sacrificially of their time and talent, even travelling to frontier areas to observe and report.

Elton Fox provided funds to invest in staff and other initiatives. Derk Van Konenynberg chaired the board for many years. Harold Gudnason, Cecil Kettle, Bob Stover, Bob Cockerell, among many others, shepherded the work through is rapid growth.

A

RT AND BETTY GEE: 1963-2000 –

We first met the Gee's when we spoke at their Chinese church in California. They graciously invited our family for lunch following the church service. Over lunch they shared, through tears, that they had committed their lives to missionary service, but after applying to two US mission agencies - and being turned down by both because they were Asian - they were discouraged.

Allen then set up an appointment with them and asked for a recommendation from their pastor. Within the next year, they joined CNEC and were assigned to Hong Kong, to develop (at that time) a new concept of youth ministries within the new Chinese speaking church plants. Their first move was to open a Youth Center, reaching College and University students. Their gifting and vision fit this need and God greatly grew that ministry. The Gee's eventually were brought back to the U.S. headquarters to work in the Chinese department, developing short term mission trips with Chinese churches.

ESTHER FAN:

Esther fled to Hong Kong from China and lived as a refugee. Esther began working with CNEC in Hong Kong and moved into leadership (1968 –1984) as CNEC Christian Education Administrator, helping with the Support -A- Child program. She also served as the Manager of the Student Center and was Assistant Coordinator from 1984-1989 for the HK/East Asia Coordinating office.

In 1989 Allen brought Esther, her husband Simon, (a pastor) and their son Ernest, to the U.S. as Ministry Coordinator to develop a Chinese Department in the U.S. headquarters. From 1989 to 2000, the Chinese Department expanded with a staff of 7 and many volunteers. Esther, having a beautiful singing voice, often sang in meetings promoting P.I. A gifted administrator and a woman of prayer, the Chinese department grew under her leadership. Under her influence, PI became known to Chinese Churches across the US. She organized prayer support for China, and the Chinese speaking world, that continues to this day.

PHIL & NANCY DEMPSTER:

I have often stated that Phil Dempster saved Allen's life. In 1976 Phil came on the staff as Vice President of Overseas Ministries. During this time, Allen was at a point of exhaustion with the responsibility for the growth and management of the mission. He needed someone to come alongside and lift the load not only for the responsibilities of the headquarters, but also for some of the burden and important overseas travel. This need was met through the arrival of Phil Dempster and his gifting for technology and the tech world, his youth, his understanding of the core ministry of PI as well as his sense of humor! Allen and Phil were a true team. He traveled the world with Allen, lifting a tremendous load from his shoulders. I am forever grateful. Phil and his wife, Nancy hail from Canada. The Dempster's now have 4 children and 7 grandchildren.

BOB SAVAGE:

Bob studied engineering when his life took a turn. God intervened and set his life in a different direction from engineering. After graduation from Fuller Seminary, Bob joined P.I. in 1986. His bent towards detail was just what P.I. needed to communicate clearly what the ministry was all about. Bob could take seemingly dull statistics from the field and create an engaging word picture in your mind and heart so that folks could understand what P.I. was all about. More importantly Bob provided a clear picture of how God was moving throughout the ministry worldwide. He updated and created new "Changing Relief and Development" reports into clear, exciting reports. He is a gifted story teller and used this gift to help others see how God  was working through P.I. throughout the world. He also was a tremendous grant writer and over the years wore many different hats in the ministry. Bob retired in 2019 and is still missed.

CARLOS CALDERON: Carlos, has been involved in PI since 1986. A man of faith, God-given understanding of indigenous leaders, patience, soft spoken, faithfulness, and a sense of humor. In the past he was Area Director for the Middle East ministries in North Africa, residing in Turkey. In

1991, he was reassigned to the U.S. headquarters as Vice President of International Ministries. Carlos and his wife are from El Salvador and have 10 children. Carlos, is a gifted leader for the P.I. ministries around the world - in 30 nations with over 300 partner ministries.

God built the staff in the U.S. Headquarters, with amazing people with special gifts, dedicated to the task of reaching for Christ those in the most difficult and restricted areas of the world. I wish there was room to write about each one but we can't or this book would be 1000 pages long. I do wish to name a few of the staff who were there in the early years as the ministry began to grow and expand. There are many more staff who had a part in establishing P.I. as the ministry grew. For all the staff we are eternally grateful to God for you.

Amy Rice 1970, Martha Barclay 1977, Marilyn Marincovich 1979, Al and Lorry Lutz 1977, Fred and Dot Simmonds, 1977, Carey Childrey 1977, Don Buchannon, Chuck Wilson

APPENDIX

A glimpse of the tremendous impact of some of Partners International ministries

PAUL CHANG: 1962 -

Paul as a young teen, with his family's blessing, fled to Hong Kong from China, with the other 1 million refugees. His father was President of the CNEC Seminary and remained in China with the rest of the family. Paul's connection with CNEC remained strong throughout those tough years. Through sponsorship Paul was able to come to the US and graduate from Seattle Pacific University. He then worked on his Seminary degree in the Bay Area. During this time we invited Paul to our home. Paul, gifted with a beautiful tenor voice, could sing as well as preach, however, his personal testimony of his survival during those early years as a refugee was something people needed to hear!

Allen could find no better person than Paul, who was the son of one of the original CNEC workers. As deputation demands grew Allen presented the opportunity to Paul and he agreed! Paul traveled for many years representing CNEC/P.I. Churches loved Paul. He became known as the Chinese Singing Ambassador. Eventually, CNEC appointed Paul to lead the ministry in Hong Kong and Southeast Asia (Malaysia, Thailand and Burma.) Paul continues in a supportive role even until today. Our girls loved "Uncle Paul" and he became part of our family. Eventually his wife, Nien Chang and their children, Mark and Ruth, joined our family.

Hong Kong – Chinese Native Evangelistic Crusade (CNEC & CNEC-HK)

The early years of CNEC in Hong Kong were very exciting. The Lord miraculously directed the leaders of CNEC to move the headquarters from China to Hong Kong in 1949. The work in China had grown even during the dark days of war and Communism until the leaders finally had to stop open ministry. The work of British missionary Fred Savage,

Calvin Chao, Dr. Andrew Song, Rev. Chang and Dr. John Kao are well documented.

The work of CNEC-HK grew tremendously in the refugee centers of Hong Kong. CNEC-HK established many schools, some of them 'roof-top' schools in the crowded high rises of the city. These grew large and influential in the rapidly developing metropolis. A large high school was begun with over 1,000 students, including a church and a clinic for outreach. Most of the schools had this 'holistic' approach that included these clinics and churches.

The vision of those original CNEC refugee pastors and HK Christian leaders was remarkable. They faced the challenge of two million refugees coming to the tiny island of Hong Kong and worked to meet the needs. Families arriving from China were destitute. Dr. Paul Chang is the son of one of the original leaders of CNEC-PI ministries in Nanking, China. Paul was only 17 when he fled with the other refugees to Hong Kong. Paul was tied to the outside of an overflowing rail car with his mother's wedding ring sewn inside his clothing. It would provide a source of funds to help him start a new life. Many pastors and workers were imprisoned in China during this time, including Paul's father.

PI began helping the church planters and sending relief for refugees. Many churches were established and in these early days, called CNEC Churches. The CNEC name is often still used.

A large SAC (Sponsor-a-Child) program was established. The government gave CNEC-HK full authorization to start schools and many 'roof top' schools were begun in the packed confines of Hong Kong. Even the infamous and lawless Walled City was not off-limits and schools and seniors were managed in this dark, chaotic den of thieves and drug dealers.

Leaders were trained at the CNEC-HK sponsored HKBS (Hong Kong Bible School) HKBS continues to graduate leaders today, often directed by second and third generation graduates. The movement spread into Singapore, Thailand, Myanmar and Malaysia with similar results.

In 2008 a conference in Indonesia brought the Hong Kong ministry full circle. One of the original CNEC churches contributed $150,000 HK dollars to the conference in this predominately Muslim country, greatly encouraging the leadership of Evangelical Theological Seminary of Indonesia, a Partners International partner ministry.

$6 to $16 Million – The Association of Chinese Evangelical Churches – Toronto

Dr. John Kao made a momentous visit to the PI office of Allen Finley in San Jose in 1978. Dr. Kao was the leader of the Hong Kong and China ministries in the early years of the mission. He and his wife Esther, a refugee child helped by child sponsorship in Hong Kong, were sensing God's call to establish churches among the thousands of Chinese preparing to leave Hong Kong for destinations around the world.

Toronto, as part of the British Commonwealth of nations, was a prime destination. Visits to Canada had shown him the need for church planting among the Chinese Diaspora.

Allen Finley made a decision to move outside the 'Policies and Procedures' of CNEC/PI and assist John to move his family to Toronto. CNEC/PI supported Dr. John for years as he began the Toronto

Chinese Community Church on Birchmount Avenue. They now number 13 congregations. One congregation is among the largest Chinese congregations in North America. They lead Canadian churches in their missions giving commitments.

Guatemala IEAL

Rev Virgilio Zapata was a well known figure in the small, Central American country of Guatemala before he began his ministry. As a skilled member of the national basketball team, he was on his way to the Olympics.

The Lord had other plans for he and his wife Bea. They saw the tremendous need for education in a country torn by violence and poverty. They began the Instituto Evangelico America Latina (IEAL) after graduating from an American seminary.

CNEC began supporting this ministry early in its history as a result of Allen Finley's personal knowledge and relationship with Virgilio. The school in Guatemala City grew to several thousand with branches in many parts of the country. Thousands of children graduate with a Christian education in this tiny country each year.

The ministry continues to grow and expand and is still supported by the UK Affiliate of PI, WorldShare. It expanded its outreach to church planting and holistic ministries, including literacy and relief during the civil war years. IEAL spearheaded the response to the massive earthquake of 1976. PI sent hundreds of thousands of dollars. The response to the earthquake almost doubled CNEC - PI's total annual income in that year.

It is difficult to find a government agency or business in Guatemala that does not benefit from the schools. Many graduates of IEAL work in offices around the country. If you visit Guatemala, you may find that the security and customs agents who process your entry are graduates. When asked "who are you going to visit", the response of "IEAL", will bring a smile and a fast track through the bureaucracy.

Liberia – Elizabeth Native Interior Mission (ENI)

Augustus (Gus) Marweih was a charismatic young man freshly graduated from the University of California at Berkley when he met Allen Finley in the early 1960's. The University of California, with dozens of campuses from San Diego to Yreka had hundreds of thousands of students on their many campuses. On the year of their 100th anniversary, they published a directory listing their top 100 students in the 100 year history. Gus Marweih was named on this list.

This was heady stuff for a young man from the deep bush of West Africa. Liberia was the least developed of all the West African nations. Gus reached the age of 14 without ever having worn clothes nor attended school! The 'white sheep' of a large family in the deep jungle, living in misery, he heard that a woman had visited the coast of Liberia and was telling people they could talk directly with the Creator. He traveled 10 days to reach the coast to hear more.

Elizabeth George, a black American missionary, met him and enrolled him in her school. Initially, he had to wear a girl's blouse to cover his nakedness at school! Gus completed his graduate studies at the University of California at Berkeley. He returned to Liberia to minister to his people in the north and eastern areas . With Partners International's help, he began a Christian school that eventually grew to train hundreds of children each year. A church planting ministry started and more than 220 churches were established in villages across Liberia. Radio ministry, prison ministry and even a program on national TV followed.

Liberia's civil war tore the country apart in the 1990's. Ten's of thousands were slaughtered. Church members fled to neighboring countries. Yet despite the upheaval, churches re-formed in camps throughout West Africa and ministered to the needy refugees.

The churches have been a positive force in the rebuilding of the country when the war ended. The churches assisted in resettling refugees, drilling wells in villages; providing medical clinics and services and caring for children orphaned in the fighting. Communities of believers continue to be established and built up across the country.

SINGAPORE BIBLE COLLEGE:
SINGAPORE Bible College (SBC)

In 1952, Dr. Calvin Chao challenged churches in Singapore to start, what today is known as the Singapore Bible College. He did this in response to the need of leadership training in Southeast Asia. PI was the only financial backer for the first seven years.

Dozens of 'CNEC' churches were established by graduates. The churches grew rapidly. Few resources existed in the nation for training pastors at a higher level.

SBC has a multi-million dollar facility in Singapore and continues to expand and produce high quality leadership throughout Asia.

The seminary is representative of scores of Bible Schools initiated and supported by CNEC since its inception. The impact of a Bible school or seminary may not be obvious but the results can multiply exponentially for generations.

Cooperacion Misionera Iberomericana (COMIBAM)

COMIBAM is one of the great milestones in the historical Christian movement. The Latin American churches saw a movement of the Holy Spirit in the early 1980's drawing them to be involved in the worldwide missions. Evidence of this movement appeared everywhere throughout Latin America. Individual churches and small agencies were springing up across the continent..

More than 500 years of Moorish rule in Spain prior to the 'discovery' of the New World gave tremendous overlap to the North Africa and Iberian cultures. Latinos had a clear call to return to North Africa and the Middle East with the good news of Jesus as the twentieth century came to a close.

Luis Bush, an Argentinean, became the Partners International Latin America Director in 1982. He pastored the Eglesia Nazaret Church in San Salvador founded by the (CAM) Central America Mission. The church was unusual in that the congregation supported dozens of missionaries throughout the world.

Luis was asked to be the International President of Partners International in 1986. While president of Partners International, he developed the concept of the '1040 Window.' This paradigm shift revolutionized mission focus to this day.

He led Partners to sponsor the first conference of COMIBAM in Sao Paulo Brazil, held in early 1987. Church leaders from across Latin America, the Iberian Peninsula and North America attended. The majority of the funding for this conference was raised by Partners International.

Alex Araujo, a Brazilian-American and the newly appointed PI Latin American Coordinator, spent 3 years from July 1986 to June 1989 in Brazil organizing the event and mobilizing Brazilian believers and local churches.

The movement of God initiated in this conference continues to this day. Churches are increasingly influenced, from Cuba to Chile. Hundreds of 'mission sending' agencies have sprung up around Latin America as a result..

Alex Araujo became the Director of International Operations at PI in the late 80's. His writings and seminars have made him the go-to expert in the area of international partnerships.

Nigeria – Gospel Light - Rev. Moses Ariye

PI had a unique role in the development of the national church in Nigeria and other parts of Africa. The African churches were exploding in the 1970's and 80's. There was a strong movement to break the colonial bonds and this movement impacted the church. Disputes between the new and rapidly growing African churches and founding missions were commonplace.

PI acted not only as an agent to empower the developing churches, but often as a peace broker between the old mission agencies and the forming ecclesiastical organizations. It was difficult for traditional missions to bridge the issues. PI offered support for national mission/church planting arms of ECWA in Nigeria (church established through the ministry of SIM International). They also performed this function with Africa Inland Church (fruit of the Africa Inland Mission) in Kenya, DR Congo, and AEF in Zambia.

PI provided support for these evangelists and church planters at 'African' levels and managed by African leadership when the mission agencies involved could not.

Moses Ariye was an unusual and gifted evangelist to the 2nd largest ethnic group in Nigeria, the Yoruba. He was often referred to as the 'Billy Graham' of West Africa because of the powerful impact he had in his campaigns to ten's of thousands across the country. He spoke to crowds of more than fifty thousand at a time. PI fully under-wrote his campaign ministry during the 1970's and 80's until his death in 1989.

Moses wrote over five hundred hymns and choruses that are still used in the large ECWA denomination of Nigeria. Fifteen hundred of his sermons were recorded for broadcast.

Brazil - EMAF – Mission to Fishermen

In 1978 Allen led a team to meet the leadership of EMAF. Marcio Garcia and his wife Demaris had begun develop this work in southern Brazil.

The remote water-accessed villages scattered along Brazil's 8,000 kilometre coastline are home to thousands of fishermen and their families. For generations, the sea has sustained them, if only by the slimmest of margins.

The Evangelical Mission for Assistance to Fishermen now has a team of more than 70 full-time

missionaries and trainees who serve the needs of these remote villages and bring the hope of the Gospel to their residents. 1300 volunteers per year work in the areas of health, community development and evangelization. 600 financial supporters have been raised up in Brazil with 7000 intercessors.

More than 2000 communities have been contacted with churches and preaching points established along the intra-coastal waterways since the ministry was initiated in the 1980's. Medical and dental teams of volunteers visit these villages periodically to provide desperately needed services to these neglected people. They now have many teams serving the lost communities in the Amazon basin along the Purus river.

EMAF began as a vision of the second generation of Canadian missionaries from the Orr family of Alberta, Canada. It took the energy, passion and anointed Marcio Garcia, a young Brazilian athlete, to move this ministry from vision to a movement of God among these neglected people.

Initially, Partners International provided close to 100% of the support needed to mobilize the Brazilians. The ministry expanded rapidly and Partners International involvement has grown dramatically over the years. Almost 90% of the resources provided for this growing ministry now come from Brazilians as the work continues to grow and expand into the Amazon Basin.

Indonesia - Evangelical Theological Seminary of Indonesia - (ETSI)

Dr. Chris Marantika studied at Dallas Theological Seminary in the late 1970's. Dr. George Peters, the renowned author and Dean of Missions at Dallas contacted Dr. Allen Finley. Dr. Peters was impressed with this Indonesian student, who showed tremendous potential as a leader of a Christian movement in that Muslim country. At the invitation of Dr. Peters, Allen Finley flew to Dallas to meet him in 1977. It was clear that he was a charismatic, focused leader who was able to clearly articulate his vision of 1:1:1. One church; in one village; in one generation.

Contrary to the principles and policies of Partners International, which dictated we should not fund a vision, PI decided to back Dr. Chris to return to Indonesia to establish a seminary. His experience with the Southern Baptists and various forms of theological education; his clear plan and the backing of all those with whom he came into contact. These observations convinced us that the vision was viable.

Dr. Greg Gripentrog, the now-retired president of One Challenge Ministries, also urged us to support Dr Chris in his vision. Along with several other mission groups, One Challenge provided personnel to teach at the seminary and guide the ministry in its formative stages. It was refreshing to deal with a Western organization that was totally committed to serving, with no concern for either control or glory.

The rest, as they say, is history. Despite flaws, mistakes and problems, the Evangelical Theological Seminary of Indonesia (STII in Indonesia) has been an extraordinary force in the expansion of the church in Indonesia. The 1:1:1 vision directly or indirectly affects many other ministries in the country. An exponential increase in evangelism and church planting across Indonesia since 1978 has been well documented.

The direct outcomes of the ministry are staggering enough. More than 4000 church plants; 31 seminaries (mini-seminaries) established in the major ethnic groups of Indonesia; a large and influential Christian university (UKRIM); Christian public schools and many related ministries.

An investigation of most major denominational and parachurch ministries will uncover graduates from ETSI across the country. The current Indonesian Minister of Religious Affairs for Protestants is an ETSI graduate. The impact on the nation has been enormous and it has the potential to continue to multiply. The concepts of church planting and evangelism among Muslims, introduced at ETSI, have been shared and incorporated in ministries in Asia and around the world.

The vision continues to grow and spread. The following is a quote from Dr. Chris Marantika in 2008; "Now 34 years have passed since Vision Indonesia 1:1:1 was born. It was like a seed that was planted 33 years ago and is now growing and scattering all over the nation. The prayers of God's people for 33 years have resulted in a tremendous outpouring of God's Spirit. In 1978, there were 20,000 churches in Indonesia. Today, 30 years later, there are more than 50,000."

Nigeria -TETMI – The Evangelisers Team Ministry

The Lord gave Rev. Sunday Umune a vision to reach rural, tribal areas among the Ibo (specifically the Edda sub-group, approximately 2 million people) that received little government assistance and less attention from the church of Christ. These were areas of intense spiritual darkness and controlling powers of evil. Some of the first missionaries to these areas were buried alive. Rev. Umune worked for three years, assisted by Partners International and saw little fruit.

In 1999 he was traveling in his car from his village to Owerri and his car was in a very serious accident with a bus. His injuries were so severe that he was still recovering two years later. On the very anniversary of the day he had the accident, the doctor removed the brace from his leg at an Orthopedic hospital in Port Harcourt. On his way back home, the bus in which he was riding struck another bus and Rev. Sunday Umune was killed, leaving his wife, Jemima and children.

His son, David Umune was already ministering in an ECWA church at this time. He sensed the Lord leading him to carry on the vision of his father to these very difficult areas under the power of the enemy.

Ministry was a hard struggle with few resources. His time was limited because of his responsibilities as pastor.

There was also something happening in the unseen world during this time. Stories that later emerged, highlighted intense battles happening among "principalities, powers, and unseen forces". Evidence of these battles could be deduced from the intense struggles of David and the Team; the unusual death of his father and the knowledge of the occult history and powerful manifestations among these tribal groups.

Some of the very overt manifestations of local spirits which confronted Jemima, the widow of Sunday Umune and to David himself showed the warfare underway in the heavenlies.

David was praying on the field during one of his visits there, for the work of TETMI, two large men, wreathed in smoke came to his door, so tall that they had to duck through the doorway of his room. They spoke and said "this is our territory." David replied "Well, that may be, but we're here now". He never saw them again

From the moment of this spiritual break-through in the ministry, things changed. Doors opened in village after village to send evangelists. Children began responding and schools started, managed by Jemima and the TETMI organization which began to see children coming to the Lord and standing against their parents when they were expected to be involved in animistic rituals.

Canadians joined in and began supporting the work. People prayed and God responded. Funds came for school building and worker support. In a few short years and after decades of struggle with little fruit, churches were planted and a ministry began to expand rapidly.

By 2008 more than 11 churches have been established with many more preaching points; 2 primary schools with some 740 kids erected. Children are taught daily from the scriptures. A high School was constructed for 140 students with lots of room for expansion and growth.

Whereas previously, gaining a foothold was a challenge, now the ministry is struggling to meet the requests and open doors that are available to them.

In recognition of his devotion to the task of world evangelism and his outstanding contribution to the mission of the Church of Jesus Christ, the participants in history's first consultation on support of indigenous ministries give special recognition and honor to

Allen Finley

as a

Pioneer and Prophet

of our movement

Charles Bennett	James Kraakevik
John C. Bennett	Bernie May
Lewis Abbott	Daniel Rickett

The Consultation Committee

The Billy Graham Center
Wheaton, Illinois
October 18, 1996

Manufactured by Amazon.ca
Bolton, ON